DARFUR
The Darfur Anthology

Acknowledgements

This project began as a discussion in the spring of 2006 between the editors and our students. We had all heard the horrific news coming out of Darfur and wanted to find a way to participate in peaceful change. When the idea of the anthology was born, we invited writers who had been guests of the Writers Center to contribute work to the project; the generosity of their response has been most gratifying.

We would like to thank the many students, faculty, administrators and staff who supported this project and assisted in production. Our special thanks go to students Jennifer Altman, Steven Evans, Christine Laspisa, Ivan Martinez, Stephanie Mitchell, Nicole Palermo, Eric Phillips, Kathryn Roberts, Landon Robins, and Rich Williamson, Deans Mary Hatch and Rick Mao, Vice President of Finance and Administration, Carole Robertson, and our President, Dr. David Sam.

Faculty Advisors
Connie Orbeta
Patrick Parks
Rachael Tecza

This printing made possible through the generous support of the Writers Center of Elgin Community College and Hagg Press, Elgin, Illinois.

Cover Design
Spartan Design Club

Graphic Design
Ivan Martinez
Nicole Palermo
Eric Phillips
Landon Robins
Rich Williamson

Table Of Contents

Holding Hope
by Ginny Knight 3

Faith
by Tim Seibles 4

conflict
by george d. clabon 6

The Soldiers
by William Heyen 7

General Romeo Dellaire, Commander of UNAIR
(United Nations Assistance Mission for Rwanda)
by David Mura 8

This Empty Place
by Leon Knight 11

The things I keep, a defense
by Bonnie Jo Campbell 12

Utensils
by Martha Cooley 17

Alchemy
by Michael Waters 18

"Your Father's Son"
by Joseph Geha 19

Elbow Room
by Leon Knight 23

Chapter Fourteen (Tradecraft)
The spring of 1986, Istanbul
by Bob Shacochis 40

Revision
by Richard Jones 49

Train To Szczecin
by Kenneth Pobo 50

The Heights of Ollantaytambo
by John Lane 51

Here
Philip Dacey 53

Eating Illinois
by Dan Guillory 54

The Plymouth
by Richard Jones 56

Molly's Bed
by Bonnie Jo Campbell 57

A language has many parts
by E. Ethelbert Miller 61

The Graduate Student's Wife
by Alice Mattison 62

Holding On
by Anne Calcagno 65

When the Universe Anoints You Master of the Obvious
by Kevin Stein 74

Title
by Richard Jones 76

Waiting for My Father to Die
by Richard Jones 77

Teacher Is Gone
by Paul Zimmer 78

Singing
by Joseph Hurka 79

Lesson
by Richard Jones 81

Working Out with Austin
by Philip Dacey 83

The Hot Stinking Truth of the Matter, or Welding Basics for Poets
by Steven Sherrill 84

Mr. A
by Frederik Pohl 88

The Plugs
by William Heyen 89

The Rape of Nanking
by David Mura 90

Four Variations on A Theme
by S.L. Wisenberg 92

Keats at Bedtime
by Philip Dacey 94

Jasmine Dream
by Kenneth Pobo 95

Glass Roots
by Kenneth Pobo 96

The Replacement Padre
by Philip Gerard 98

Day of the Dead: This Time
by Barry Silesky 108

A Fable with a Photograph of a Glass Mobile on the Wall
by Kevin Brockmeier 110

Elegy for a Limb
by Kenneth Pobo 116

Escape to Olmstead Road
by Bonnie Jo Campbell 117

Change the World
by Cris Mazza 119

Things One Does Not Regret
by David Mura 133

The hostage husband
by E. Ethelbert Miller 134

Circus Animal
by E. Ethelbert Miller 135

Untitled
by G.W. Clift 136

Wind Thinks
by Kenneth Pobo 145

Letter to Laura
by Elizabeth Searle 146

Fruit
by E. Ethelbert Miller 150

Machete Season
by David Mura 151

History Book
by Ginny Knight 155

Villanelle for Distant Strangers
by Patricia Monaghan 156

The Planets
by Richard F. Gillum 157

Contributor's Notes

Kevin Brockmeier 158

Anne Calcagno..158

Bonnie Jo Campbell 158

george clabon 159

G.W. Clift 159

Martha Cooley 159

Philip Dacey 159

Joe Geha..159

Philip Gerard 160

Richard F. Gillum 160

Dan Guillory 160

William Heyen 161

Richard Jones..161

Ginny Knight 161

Leon Knight 162

John Lane 162

Alice Mattison 162

Cris Mazza...162

E. Ethelbert Miller 162

Patricia Monaghan 163

David Mura..163

Kenneth Pobo 163

Frederik Pohl 164

Elizabeth Searle 164

Tim Siebles..164

Bob Shacochis...165

Steven Sherrill 165

Barry Silesky...165

Kevin Stein..166

Michael Waters 166

S.L. Wisenberg 167

Paul Zimmer 167

Foreword

Darfur.
Over 200,000 dead! And counting!!
Over 2 million displaced! And counting!!
Every girl and woman at risk of rape!!!

As I flew over Africa during spring break 2007 to visit my native country, Ghana, I couldn't help reflecting on the tragedy in Darfur. What if my destination had been Darfur, Sudan, and not Ghana? Would I have found any relative there? Maybe not; they would probably have been part of the statistics mentioned above. And so it is for the people of Darfur since 2003.

Darfur, the tragedy of the day, the genocide of the day, does not seem to have a voice. But, in reality, the people of Darfur have more than enough voices around the world. What they have lacked is the will on the part of world leaders to stop the counting of dead bodies in Darfur.

I wonder what it will take to wake these leaders from their deep slumber. After relatively recent genocides in Cambodia, Bosnia, Rwanda, etc., the world seemed to have said "never again." How soon we forget! Back then, some even claimed that they were not aware of what was happening in these countries. Today, no one can claim they are unaware of this tragedy unless they pretend it does not exist. And isn't that what some leaders are doing?

But Darfur will not go away quietly. Unfortunately, the counting continues while the world political leadership sleeps. Thankfully, the next victims in Darfur have voices: voices of hope that their plight will not be forgotten. And that is what this book is about. In a very small way, these writers are determined to keep the Darfur genocide on the front pages and on the minds of all with the hope that the counting will end. I thank all of the writers for giving voices to the dying children, women, and men of Darfur. To the faculty members at Elgin Community College involved in this project, I commend you for your passion and activism. Knowing of the College's involvement in this attempt to throw a brighter light on the Darfur tragedy is so far the highlight of my tenure at the institution.

David Fiifi Sam, Ph.D., J.D.
President
Elgin Community College

Holding Hope

by Ginny Knight

'tired of taking fear and calling it life'
from *broken and Beirut*
by Suhzir Hammad of Palestine

who named the world
    earth
broke it into
    tribes
    clans
made language secret
    dividing
    separating
imprisoning us in fear
    exiled
who names revenge
    takes fear
    calls it life

who names the stars
    moon
    sun
removes fear from
    earth
    sky
    universe
holds reverence in life
    mysterious
    sacred
in these numbered days
    who
    holds out hope...

Faith

by Tim Seibles

Picture a city in flames
and the survivors: some scream
from their windows, some walk
stunned, looking around: blood and still
more blood   coming
from the mouth of a girl.

This is the same movie
that has been playing all over
the world: starring everybody
who ends up where the action is: lights,
cameras, shrapnel and extreme
close-ups of what used to be somebody's leg.

Stop talking about *God*. Shut-up
about heaven: some of our friends
who should be alive   are no longer alive.
Moment by moment death moves
and memory doesn't remember.

Even today– even having said
this, even knowing that
someone is stealing
our lives-- I have had a big lunch
and bought new shoes.

Tell the truth. If you can.
Does it matter   who they were,
the bodies in the rubble: could it matter

that we're all conceived by two people
buried in each other's arms, believing
completely   in the world between them?

The commanders are ready. The killers
are everywhere. They all believe
in God: who, according to

The Silence, must believe
in them. But somebody should
hold a note   for the Earth--

a few words for whatever it could mean
to remain human beneath the forgotten sky:

some day one night,
when the city lights go out for good,

you won't believe how many stars

conflict

by george d. clabon

i hear the voices
       carried by the wind
       calling out for change
to how we settle
       conflict

always at the end
       of barrel
some sort of another
       spilling life
       instead of living
       life
in shared spaces

       calling for change
the wind carries voices
       i hear
on how we settle
       conflict....

The Soldiers

by William Heyen

In Afghanistan, Taliban soldiers have reduced an ancient Buddhist temple to rubble & have covered stones with graffiti. "We confront the idols of non-Muslims and destroy them," one soldier says.

A famous clay-baked statue of Buddha is beheaded & hacked into thousands of pieces. "The Buddha was here, but we have smashed it," another soldier says.

But where the Buddha was, the Buddha is, 170' high in a sandstone cliff or engrained on a grain of rice. The wise of all religions know this, & know that cliffs are dust & pumice, rice food for meditation, & know that Buddha, Jesus, Mohammed knew/know this. Rondure & sungleam, central belly & windflow form, the enlightened one is benign presence even in the cold sweat & seed of the benighted soldiers.

Explosives explode two huge 3rd & 5th Century Buddhas. Each particle is of the whole, trillions of Buddhas for brain & bloodstream.

O soldiers, with every breath you breathe them in. Even today, they are born forever again in your children who will some day not be able—will they?—to honor or even remember you.

General Romeo Dellaire, Commander of UNAIR
(United Nations Assistance Mission for Rwanda)

by David Mura

I
"Rwanda? That's in Africa, isn't it?"
The words of a nitwit; an incompetent fool.
Now it's a trace deep in my nostrils.
Each scent finds a face, a flashback, a codicil.

Whatever my father taught me as a soldier,
whatever his father taught him,
neither taught me the art of memory--
How to forget or just let it dim.

II
I saw a Hutu girl pick her way down the road,
her faultless dark skin, her light dress in the sun.
She passed a truck stuffed with the vanished. Tripped
in a puddle. Her light dress stained by mud.

But when she looked down her mouth pierced the air
and the more she screamed and recoiled,
the more passersby stopped to stare--
Someone had soaked her dress in dark red oil.

III
There was a rat the size of a terrier.
We all knew the flesh he'd been seizing.
Today in the grocery I picked up a guava.
The bodies before me, the market of Kigali.

Many nights I'm on the phone to someone I know.
They're pleading for help, pleading their life.
Over and over I tell them wait, help will come....
Screams. Shots. Silence of a dead line.

III

I close my eyes and see a baby wiggling
beside the bloated body of his mother.
I pick up the tingly and mushy being:
What twitches there is a feast of maggots.

And even when the maggots jawed their fill
and skeletons bleached to white in the sun,
the images seared my cortex—Her bone legs
bent apart. A broken bottle between them.

V

Near the end I brought some goats to the compound.
I watered and fed them and they roamed the grounds.
I wanted to believe I could at least save them.
Wild dogs from the streets would not take them down.

And when the dogs breached the fences I was there;
I sprinted across the lawn and emptied my clip.
I missed those son of a bitches but they did run.
Turned to the faces of my men. They knew I'd lost it.

VI

Yes, the army asked me to rest, to stop my testimony.
I thought if I shed my uniform my soul might return.
I am still waiting—I let men die, women and children.
My boys, my soldiers, those smart ass Belgians.

(Kill the white man with the mustache,
kill Dellaire, Hutus shouted on the radio.
I knew any white soldier could be my double.
And still I ordered them out on patrol.)

VII

If only I'd hit a mine or run to an ambush,
If only I'd joined those whom I failed.
If only I'd attacked against my orders.
If only I'd run the risk of jail.

And if Colonel Teoneste Bagarosa
and others are now shut up in quiet cells?
What comfort is that to the voices of Darfur?
Please shut the door again. It's noisy, sirs, here in hell.

VIII
I am General Romeo Dellaire. Once upon a time I was a soldier.

This Empty Place

by Leon Knight

This empty place
cannot be filled
      with tears
      or rage
or communion wine.
I cannot run
      fast enough
      or far enough.
Now
with nothing left,
      I must look
at this empty place.
Finally
I realize
      I must live...
with this empty place
      always looking
      back at me.

The things I keep, a defense

by Bonnie Jo Campbell

Each year I clean out the pan cupboard—that's the lower right cupboard when you're standing at the sink. Each year I consider getting rid of the crepe pan, which we have never used. Each year I take it out and hold it up by its solid wooden handle and look through the dime-sized in the sides, and then I decide to keep it. It is made well and feels good in my hand. I could be a person who make crepes: cheese or fruit, or cheese and fruit together. "Get rid of that thing," Christopher says. "But it was your dad's," I protest. I put it back under the cupboard. I didn't keep everything we inherited from John Magson. For ages I've stored his kitchen table in the attic, but most of those little matchstick chairs had broken beneath American weights and we burned rather than repaired the remnants. I did keep his denim cooking apron, which I wore yesterday to make a peach pie for my brother Tom, using one of my granny Betty's old pie pans.

Once the crepe pan goes back into the cupboard for another year, we forget about it, and the quart-sized yogurt containers are more likely then to become a point of contention, because they sit in the front in stacks and fall out when we open the cupboard doors. Even I am not sure why I want to keep a hundred quart-sized plain yogurt containers, except that I suspect there is some use for them. I fear that one week after I throw them away, somebody will say, "Oh, we could have used those to save lives." To be honest, though, the only use I've so far found for them (apart from storage) is to put the toilet brush in beside the toilet.

For years I kept milk jugs, hundreds of them, all with their lids on, strung together on baling twine. I wanted to build a raft out of them and float down the St. Joseph River during the Venetian festival in St. Joe. But then they cancelled the flotilla event—apparently too many drunken rowdy people on the water was a liability. Still, for a long time I considered just making a raft for my own adventure. I would wear a crown and call myself the dairy princess and launch at Scottdale. I would bring my friend Jamie Blake with me and a bottle of wine (or a jug of Kaluha and cream), and we would each have a canoe paddle, and we would wave at everyone we saw on shore as we floated past. Just thinking about that lost dream makes me a little sad that this spring I finally recycled all those milk bottles, clearing them out of the attic and the shed. That recycling day was when I first noticed the woodchuck holes in the dirt floor of the shed.

Like a good farm girl, I save canning jars, and any glass jar that takes a standard sized lid is classified as a canning jar. That includes mayonnaise jars, Marie's salad dressing jars, and some peanut butter jars. In my opinion, all jars should take standardized lids—it should be a law. And in fact that would help cut down on the clutter in my lid drawer—yes, I have a lid drawer. If lid sizes were standardized, if I could count on any given lid fitting any given jar, then I wouldn't have to keep so many. I now recycle many of the non-standardized jars, unless they're particularly attractive, such as the Dundee marmalade jars or the decorative jelly jars, in which case I save them for use as drinking glasses. And maybe we already have a few too many glasses and cups (they don't all fit into the cupboard at one time), but if we had fewer, then we'd have to do the dishes more often than we do.

In the cupboard on the other side of the sink, there are a lot of canned goods. I repeat, *a lot* of canned goods. We have no basement for shelter during national emergency, but we will not die from starvation, at least not for a while. Food doesn't count as clutter, especially not canned food, which does not need to be managed and rotated like the meat and fresh fruit and vegetables crammed into our European-sized refrigerator (a refrigerator made for those people meant to sit in those matchstick chairs we got from John Magson). I'm not so careful with cheese, however, because you can just cut off the mold. Christopher does not subscribe to this theory of moldy cheese, however, which means I have to cut off the mold before I bring cheese to the lunch table.

The fruit and vegetables require constant vigilance, but I've been pretty lax about my own garden tomatoes in the last few weeks. Christopher is very distressed about the ones currently rotting atop the refrigerator. I will take care of them soon. I want to go through them carefully, as there might be good ones in the bunch; though to be perfectly honest, one bad tomato often does ruin the whole bunch. At this time of year, in the garden, the proportion of good tomatoes to bad dwindles.

For the record, Christopher's claim that I have 72 bottles of shampoo is a gross exaggeration. First of all, the number of bottles is only 33 (I'm not going to count the hotel-sized bottles), and second of all, half of those bottles are conditioner. That's all I'm going to say about that stuff in the bathroom.

We all need more beauty in our lives. Throwing away anything beautiful would be wrong, so how can I throw away the wrapping paper that my friends chose so carefully? Someday I may want to give a gift that is not just stapled into a paper bag, and I could re-use some of this beautiful wrapping paper. And what about greeting cards? Do people really just throw them away? I know it's the thought that counts, the fact that those people actually remembered my birthday, and I ought to be able to hold onto that long after I've tossed away the card. Except that my memory is so lousy that without the card I won't remember who gave me a card. And some of those cards are really touching and funny, like the one Heidi just gave me with the little girl wearing giant wax lips.

I recall the way my grandfather Frank Herlihy's life ground nearly to a halt as a result of all his stuff. Once he turned about 88 years old, it would go like this: he would go into the living room to get something; he would get distracted by an old letter or a book he'd read as a youth or by a trinket he'd given his wife Betty, then he'd stop what he was doing and ponder the object, reconsider all its meaning and be almost paralyzed by memories. That's how I want to be when I am old and alone and ill, surrounded by objects that are drenched with meaning, objects with the potential to stop time. The alternative, of course, is to be old and alone and ill without anything you love to distract you.

Frank Herlihy's woodpiles were something of a travesty in those last years, however. Most of the wood was spongy and moss covered. Christopher has been on me lately to get rid of some of the wood I've been saving, and so I've disassembled my mammoth woodpile and am letting him burn whatever is moss-covered or moldy or spongy (though I could save half of many of those pieces, since only half the length of many is spongy or moss covered). I'm throwing short pieces onto the fire just because they are short, that's how far I'm going! I've got only a rowboat-sized pile left, and I've put a tarp on it. Christopher says that most of those pieces are no good because they've got nails in them. I've promised that if he needs a piece, I will pull the nails out. He says the nails are probably rusted in. I suspect that Frank Herlihy would have pulled the nails out before putting the wood on the pile.

I haven't even addressed the other woodpile, the woodpile inside the shed, containing clean dry wood, oak tongue-and-groove- floorboards and odd 1x4 lengths we used for window and door trim. Ever since the woodchuck took up residence in the shed, I've dreaded working in there. I know we should shoot the woodchuck, but getting rid of the living creatures can be even more difficult than getting rid of inanimate stuff. Maybe just maybe that woodchuck has a purpose in the scheme of things. He's very cute when he suns himself in our backyard, and he seems to enjoy his life a great deal. As do the spiders living in both our bathrooms.

The stray cats are another problem. I don't think the hungry flea-ridden beasts enjoy their lives immensely, but there they are. We don't want them here, because the wild birds enjoy their lives much less (or for a much shorter period of time) when the cats are around. The mamma cat with her seven babies was not enjoying her life much when we discovered her, though the little tiger kittens were irresistible. What mama did with food could not be classified by anyone as enjoyment. She devoured food, inhaled food, attacked food, and turned it into milk. I did not want to keep those cats in a cage on the porch, but I had to keep them there until they could get on the path to a life in somebody's home, which they did after a month.

Old paint cans. Now there's something I've explained to Christopher numerous times. You have to keep what's left of the paint from each room so that you can touch up your paint when the metal futon bangs against the wall or when a greasy handprint appears. And that is why I have all those one-gallon each containing three ounces of whitish paint. And since it's all latex, we can't store it outside—latex can't take the freezing and thawing. Normal people would keep this paint in the basement, of course, but again, we haven't got a basement.

Though I've filled my office with floor to ceiling bookshelves, space is in short supply, and most of my shelves have books sitting horizontally on the tops of the vertically arranged books. I've considered getting rid of some of my math books, though doing so now while I'm writing a novel about mathematics would seem foolish: who knows which one I might need for reference. I suppose I don't really need more than a few composition textbooks, and probably two writing usage handbooks would answer all my questions, but sometimes a particular rule is stated better by one author than another.

My files. You might think I don't need a file for each one of my friends and family members, but if I didn't then where would I file those thoughtful, sometimes hilarious, birthday cards? And you might think I don't need a file for each state I've visited, but then it is awfully handy to have the "Indiana" folder when it's time to go to Jasper Pulaski State Game Area to see the Sandhill Cranes, to find the directions and the phone number so we can call and find out what percentage of the Eastern United State's population of cranes is currently sleeping there (by mid November it approaches 9% of the Eastern Population)

I sift through my clothes every year, and each year I manage to get rid of a few things. This summer in a reckless bout of confidence, I actually tossed away three pairs of pants that fit me when I'm 30 lbs heavier. I've been considering getting rid of the pants for years, but boy oh boy will I feel dumb if I gain the weight back. I rarely have to buy shirts, as people usually give them to me. I still have the red softball-type shirt that my staff at the high school newspaper the "Round-Up" gave me in 1980. "Editor" it says on one side and "Fish" it says on the other—that was my nickname. I'd wear it but it's a little tight in the armpits.

Refugees are driven from their homes every day, torn asunder from their lives and their home and their belongings. Sometimes over decades some aspects of life can be rebuilt, but the beloved things, from past generations, from friends, from family are all gone forever. To get rid of stuff I loved out of misguided principles of austerity might be to make myself a refugee in my own home. I won't do it. Instead I will revel in the privilege of staying put and I will revel in the accumulation of things that matter to me.

I think I really will make crepes this year, but for now I'll put this pan back with my other pans, including the big non-stick pan Sheila and Matt gave me a few years ago, the pan I still cook in everyday. I can feed them some crepes. Fifteen years ago my mother Susanna gave me that ancient cast-iron corn muffin pan which makes muffins in the shape of cobs of corn, More recently, Christopher gave me one like it with the shape of fish. That enameled Dutch oven that Susanna gave me has been my fudge-making pan for the last six years—I've considered getting a more appropriate pan, one made out of a newfangled material I've read about, but the longer I make candy in this one, the more difficult it is to change it.

In a more practical defense of clutter, I will say that, with all I have here, I have what I need. I may even have what you need, and I invite you to come over and borrow it. I may even give it to you. At midnight last night when David Magson said he needed a table for his computer, without hesitation I dragged in the ladder, got up in the attic and extricated the big wooden table from in and around the boxes of dishes, old mirrors, a disassembled double bed, computer cartons. How perfect is that? He now has a table that belonged to his own father! I handed him down the legs, then the big table top. Susanna said she needs a printer; no problem—I've been saving my old laser printer. It works beautifully so long as you just feed it one piece of paper at a time. So stop by if you need something, and we can interest you in a big neutered male gray long-haired cat? He's free to a good home.

Utensils

by Martha Cooley

FORK

Use the tines to spear a plump
illusion. (Pick your favorite.)
Lift it to your mouth; bite into it.
Feel the delectable spurt
as it ruptures.

KNIFE

Hold it sharp edge down,
angling the blade. Slice off
a solid chunk of whatever it is
you think you have to have.
Slide the blade beneath;
raise it up, then drop it
onto your waiting tongue.
Begin to chew.
You'll be at it a long while.

SPOON

Use its stiff tip to prise off the lid.
Scoop the dark contents
into a cup. Ladle hot milk
plus sugar, a pinch of salt; stir.
Lap up this porridge (a little
bitter, no?). Then think
how you must have been fed, mouthful
by mouthful, when you were young,
a diet of deepest longing.
Reckon with the aftertaste,
a faint residual sweetness.

Alchemy

by Michael Waters

Familiar words suddenly became strange,

Confusing him—not so much their meanings,

But their characters, the letters themselves—

Some quirk of the eyesight, less a loss

Of language than its transformation,

Ovidian, the marks writhing while read,

Poetry, perhaps, bewitched to *burlap*:

The *p* suddenly tumbled upside down,

The clasps of *o* and *e* opened—*u r*—

Then the *t-r-y* become *l-a-p*

Uncrossed, doubled up, pinched shut faced forward

Respectively, devilishly—the word

Less abstract, assuming texture and heft,

Rough to the touch, less a bolt of lightning

Than bolt of cloth woven to bind the book.

"Your Father's Son"

by Joseph Geha

Say-leem? *S'l-eem? Suh-leem?* Over and over during Sam's first months in America Sister Mary Celestine kept having to ask how to pronounce his name. He'd been entered directly into the first grade at Saint Francis School on Cherry Street, where every day seemed to bring a new bewilderment. So much so that Sister eventually declared him to be "slow as molasses." Whatever molasses was. Eventually, with the calling of each morning's roster his own true name, pronounced reluctantly and with baffled misprecision, had begun to sound more and more foreign, even to himself.

Some days he found himself near to crying, but about what exactly he couldn't quite say. He remembered sitting there, trying to make sense of the sounds that leaped out of Sister's rapid drone--*wha ... isst ... haow ... plok ... wha...*, and just like that he would feel it begin in his throat, a choking which he ahemed and ahemed against until the struggle itself shook the sobs out of him, releasing them rhythmically, like hiccups. Heads turned: he was at it again, the big kid in back who cried at nothing. Their fair, puzzled little faces, some of them genuinely concerned: What is it? His eyes blurred, but the tears never came, only the choking. Some time after Christmas, it was during one of these episodes that Sister Celestine, yardstick in hand, strode down the aisle to the last row, bent over him and through her gritted teeth uttered the first ever complex English sentence that he would understand completely: *You stop that crying right now or I'll give you something to cry about!*

At home — in the flat above the store — his mother stayed all day alone, cooking, praying her rosary in the window, bottling up her aloneness, and as soon as Baba closed for the night, she would open up, even as he was climbing the stairs. "How can *this* be America?" She would ask. Each time Baba seemed taken by surprise, furrowing his brow in bewilderment. He had no answer. He sat himself wearily into the blue velvet armchair while Sam knelt to unlace his father's shoes. Mornings before dawn Baba left them asleep and drove off to the wholesale markets; even by the time he had come back and opened the store, it would still be dark out. He ate his lunch in the store, and Mama carried his supper down to him. Some afternoons she came downstairs to sit with him, but because of her reluctance to learn English or to cipher English numbers, she was of little use behind the counter. Better she stay upstairs than down here, her eyes following him from butcher block to cash register, the whole time accusing him, as if America had put no roof over her head, no food on her table, provided no schooling for her son.

Because English was such a struggle at first, Sam was forced to repeat his first year. All the following summer he spent mornings being tutored. Soon he found himself letting Arabic go, gradually, and quite deliberately. He resolved to speak only English, even at home. This new-found determination helped ease his shame as he watched last year's kindergartners file in and take seats at the desks around him: after all, now he too spoke nothing but English, like them. Still, they were so young looking, and small-built. He had grown taller over the summer. Hulking over his little desk, he felt like a bear.

"Say-loum? Saah-lim?" Sister still couldn't get it right.

Among the *ibn Arab*, names are at once both simple and complicated, important and unimportant. According to tradition, a man who has a firstborn son names him after his own father, the boy's grandfather. He was named Saleem, for instance, after Baba's father; in turn, his own firstborn son would be named Rasheed, after Baba, and his son's son Saleem after himself, and so on. But by an odd wrinkle of tradition, as soon as you have a son and name him after your father, your own name becomes unimportant and you give it up to become known in the community as simply the father of your son. Upon Sam's birth, Baba was no longer Rasheed and became known as *abou Saleem*. The father of Saleem. But since Saleem was also Baba's father's name, in a way he was also his father's father. Tangled and mixed, no wonder a favorite Arabic endearment was *ya ba'adi*, oh part-of-me.

Here in America, though, things were different. Here, some decided, it was best to carry an American name. Sam, for instance, instead of Saleem. It was just good business. His father would understand that. At Sunday dinner, his parents sat listening, but he had barely begun to explain –– "None of the Americans call Baba Rasheed. To them he's Shade..."–– when Mama raised her eyebrows and waved the whole business off with a quick, backward swipe of both hands. In English it would be like a shrug. Then she stood up to clear the dishes. Sam looked across the table at his father.

"Sam?" Baba said. He too raised his eyebrows and shrugged, but American style, with the shoulders. "Okay." Then he nodded, pulling down the corners of his mouth into the face he made whenever he closed a deal.

That was easy. But then again his parents never used his name much anyway, rarely called him Saleem. In fact, they called him everything but his name. In Arabic children were smothered with endearments: *ya habeebi*, oh my beloved one; *ya ahlbi*, oh my heart; *ya adahmi*, oh my bones; and one of Mama's favorites, *ya rohi*, oh my life-breath.

Saleem? What was that to his mother and father? No name could compare to *ya tibourini*, the ultimate parental endearment, *Oh you who will bury me*.

*

At end of the second year at Saint Francis, Sam was reading well beyond his grade level. Again and again he began to catch himself actually thinking in English. Baba began bragging about him to customers in the store. His pride was so unrestrained, in fact, that Sam was often startled by it. He might be passing behind the cash register on his way to sort empty soda-pop bottles, and suddenly an arm would sweep him up to show him off. The customer, usually one of the *ibn Arab*, would smile fondly and say *Is'mallah alek, ya ibn Rasheed*, naming him the son of his father. And ibn Rasheed, face flushing, he would have to nudge his father please to stop. After all, English was *easy* now, reading and writing and speaking, all of it unbelievably easy. His embarrassment, of course, was all surface; down deep he was thrilled, even as Baba continued to embrace him. Sam would always remember his father's smell as the smell of work, raw meat from the butcher block, cigars, the sawdust on his heavy brogan lace-ups, and beneath it all that unmistakably sweetish redolence to his body that later, in medical school, he would learn to associate with cancer.

*

His mother rarely dared step out into the world beyond the North End; after all, what if she got on the wrong bus? She might have to talk to an American!

Not speak Engleezi! she would complain if an American said the least thing to her.

Don't forget your change, Ma'am.

Not speak Engleezi!

Good morning!

Not speak Engleezi!

In the North End there were plenty of women — Aunt Libby for one — who had come here from the old country believing that in America you make your own luck by rolling up your sleeves and working elbow to elbow with the men. It was the American way: you learned the money first and then the language, and then you depended on nobody. But there also were women like Sam's mother who, in their hearts never really left the remote hill villages where they had been born. Married off as children practically, to men twice their age, these had become widows in their forties. In their fifties they were like old people. Poorly schooled, if at all, they centered their lives upon their children and the Church and, increasingly, television. They didn't drive cars, of course, and since they could barely communicate with bus drivers, their children wound up having to drive them whenever they left the North End.

But over the years, and in spite of themselves, they did come to speak a kind of English. Kneading dough at the kitchen counter, Sam's mother would sometimes parrot radio jingles that for some reason must have caught her fancy: "Two full glasses dhaz a lot!" from the Pepsi Cola jingle and "Now, Stella Dallas," from

the soap opera and "Okay, Louie, drop da gun, you not foolin' anyone," from --
God only knew where that came from. In time so many English words and phrases
had crept so gradually into her speech that she ended up speaking an Arabic that
virtually was English, pronounced with a heavy accent and the attachment of
Arabic word endings. And the odd thing, Sam believed, wasn't that most Americans
could figure out this patois fairly easily, nor that newcomers from the old country
could barely recognize it as Arabic; it was that Mama, and the others like her,
hardly recognized that a change had even occurred. They thought they were still
speaking Arabic when they said "*Dahrivni al stahrr*" for "Drive me to the store."

    And driven to the store they had to be. Their mail had to be read to them,
notices from the city translated for them, their bills paid, the checks filled in for
them above the careful looping of their illiterate signatures. But soon the neighborhoods of Little Syria began to dissolve. As their children grew and began
venturing out into the Greater America beyond, the lives of these women became
increasingly difficult. To meet their simplest needs, they had to navigate daily the
guilty waters between gratitude and resentment. (*A mother's heart pours itself out
solely upon her child*, the Arabic saying goes, one of his mother's favorites, *while the
child's heart pours itself out upon the stones of the world.*) And because they had
learned to do so little for themselves, many of them remained, for their children,
impossible to leave. Every one of these households had at least one grown,
unmarried child.

*

    Older than Mama by almost thirty years, Baba lived a long life and, like most
rascals, he died old.   After the funeral, lying awake in bed Sam could hear his
mother in the bedroom next to his, muttering English words in her sleep; she who
never learned English, who never learned to do the bills, the shopping, the driving around; who couldn't answer a phone. All her life married to an old man.
What had Sam expected? He'd somehow always known that Baba would eventually be leaving her to him.

The End

Elbow Room

by Leon Knight

The stocky old man hung up the phone and said, "He can bring your tire when he delivers mail tomorrow. Your best bet is a good used one. . . . So, I told him to bring that."

The woman nodded glumly. "We only got two or three hundred miles to where his dad is. But we need four good tires."

"Yup. You're lucky that spare got you this far. Twenty miles was about all it could do."

"Well, as long as this one will get us to his dad." She perked up a bit' and looked at him across the counter. "Did you say the mailman's delivering it?"

"Yup. He comes this way three days a week. If we need something special, we call him, and he'll throw it in the back of his truck."

"And you pay the postage when he gets here?"

"Naw. It's got nothing to do with the post office. He's just being neighborly . . . since he's coming this way anyway. Might slip him a few bucks now and then . . . Just to be neighborly back."

"So, me and Joe just pay him for the tire, with a few neighborly dollars thrown in."

"That's about it." He extended his hand across the counter. "My name's Whitey."

She returned his grip. "I'm Sparkle. That's my grandson Joe." She nodded her head towards the sleepy young man on the last stool with his head down on the counter.

"Your grandson?" Whitey asked skeptically.

Sparkle grinned. "Can't a black woman have a Mexican grandson?"

Then she explained - "He started calling me Grandma. . . you know, to tease me where we worked at the deli back in Chicago. So I'd say back, 'Be a good boy and do what Grandma tells you'. . . After awhile, we'd say it, even when we weren't fooling around. . . So, here we are."

Whitey nodded - "Yup. Here you are."

Then he asked, "You want something to eat?"

"I better save what little money we got left. There's a bit of food left in our stash. I'll heat some up when we set up camp tonight."

"Who said anything about money? . . .Do you want something to eat?"

Her eyes snapped. "We don't need charity."

He stiffened too. "Who said anything about charity? I was just being neighborly."

She softened instantly and, after a moment, softly said, "That sounds good . . . Let me wash up first." She looked around for the rest rooms.

The old man pointed. "The key's by the door. It's around the side."

She was back in a minute. "Whitey, you got any cleaning stuff? That women's room is nasty."

* * * * *

When she came back inside, Whitey was dealing with an irate customer. Joe, with his head still on the counter, was enjoying the show.

From behind the main register near the front door, the old man calmly but firmly explained, "It ain't my fault your credit card is maxed out."

The middle-aged man, whose years were emphasized by his failed attempt to look younger, snarled, "What kind of place doesn't have an ATM these days?"

"My kind of place. We ain't Wal-Mart. And we don't take checks. . . . That'll be thirty-eight dollars, please."

The man was defiant - "And what could you do about it if I just drove off?"

"I wouldn't do nothing . . . except phone the patrol. With that kid-car you're driving and a New Jersey license plate, you'd have to stay on the blacktop. That's forty miles before you can turn off the way you're headed, and farther than that if you turn around. The patrol would get you either way."

The man slapped two bills down on the counter and muttered - "That just leaves me two dollars in cash."

Whitey forced a straight face as he gave the man his change. "There's a Wal-Mart with an ATM a couple miles beyond that first turnoff I mentioned."

Hating being bested by an an old country-hick, the man snarled, "And what would you do if I got my gun?"

"Oh, I don't think you'd do that. . . not for thirty-eight dollars. But if . . ." Keeping his eyes on the man, Whitey reached under his counter and pulled up a short-barreled automatic shotgun.

The man's eyes widened before he raced to his car. The other three watched until they heard his tires squeal as they hit the blacktop of the highway.

The old man, who had already returned the shotgun to its place, grinned sheepishly and said, "I wouldn't a done nothing if he pulled a gun. There's nothing here worth shooting for."

The boy asked, "But what about your shotgun?"

"I use it to keep the wild jackasses south of the road. A couple of blasts will usually scare them off."

In response to the woman's unasked question, Whitey added, "I'll tell you about it sometime."

After returning the cleaning equipment to the storeroom, Sparkle came out with some other supplies and went behind the counter. "I don't know about you men," she groused. "That men's room was even worse . . . If 'cleanliness is next to Godliness', God must be a woman."

She began scraping the top of the grill.

Joe grinned and said to Whitey, "That's just the way Grandma is - nothin' was ever clean enough for her at the deli."

"That's true," Sparkle admitted, as she turned to smile tenderly at the boy. "You may be a work-in-progress, but you are getting better."

He just grinned in response.

* * * * *

Across the front of the building was a covered porch - covered to keep the direct sun off of the windows and occasional loungers, and a porch only if wooden planks thick enough to elevate it above the mud when it did rain could be called a porch. The treated planks extended around the end of the building to become a sidewalk back to the rest rooms.

The corner was widened and extended, with a railing on the outside. This corner with two wicker chairs and a small table was Whitey's favorite place to sit during the long twilight and early dark.

The lighted "pay at the pump" sign to attract passing motorists was off the other end of the station and, with only night lights on inside, Whitey's corner became almost completely dark after the sun finally set.

That's where Sparkle found him that evening. The motion light came on as she walked by the rest rooms.

"Come and join me," the old man said. "There's coffee in the pot."

She didn't ask him why he had a second mug on the tray.

As she filled her cup and topped his, she said, "I'm so sleepy tonight that caffeine this late won't keep me awake."

"The room's all right, then?"

"Compared to sleeping in a tent, it's great. I'm on the bed, and Joe's got both air mattresses blown up for himself . . . He's pleased you've got a satellite dish. He was flipping through the channels when I left."

The motion light went off.

In the dusk, Whitey said, "He's a good boy . . . We'll put his car on the hoist tomorrow to check it over before you get back on the road."

"He told me," the woman said. "That's really nice . . . And the use of your room."

"Just being neighborly," the old man said. "The room's just sitting there . . . That TV set in your room belongs to a woman who used to work for me . . . running the lunch counter. But she moved on."

Sparkle was surprised - "Why did she leave a nice little set like that behind?"

"The trucker she left with already had TV in his sleeping cab. She said she'd pick it up sometime, but she never did."

After a moment, Sparkle said, "Well, maybe she will."

"Yup, maybe she will."

They sat in silence until the sun was a faint glow silhouetting the distant mountains. Leaning back in her chair, the woman looked up at the night sky and softly said, "Man, I can see why you named this place Elbow Room."

"It had that name when I showed up fifteen years ago. Eva's husband named it when he bought it. But he did get it right. . . . He died about three years before I came down the road."

"And you got the place from her?"

"No. She still owns it, I guess . . . I just took over the garage and gas station part, which was too much for her alone . . . That's when I finished the room you're in . . . Thought I'd be here a month or two . . . six months top."

The woman looked his way and hesitantly said, "And you're still here fifteen years later . . . What about Eva?"

After a long pause, his voice came through the darkness - "She's buried back up close to the draw. Just over two years ago. . . There are some trees there. . . Still mean to put up a fence. . . to keep the jackasses from walking all over her. . . But I don't know . . . I may be getting too old for that."

"Yeah," she said sympathetically, understanding now why he, a man who had nothing in the store worth shooting for, kept his shotgun handy by the cash register.

* * * * *

The next morning, Sparkle prepared to fix breakfast, starting with coffee from her own dwindling supply. "I like to grind it each morning," she said to Whitey. "But we didn't have room in the car for my mill. So I ground what I had for the trip."

The old man raised his cup in appreciation and said, "Sure beats what I make."

"Wait'll you taste her omelets," Joe said eagerly. "She's famous for them. And I made sure we had room for her spices."

"The eggs are in the bottom of the 'fridge," Whitey suggested.

"Already found 'em. And some potatoes. . . . Do you prefer hash browns or country fries?"

"Country fries," Joe said eagerly.

"I wasn't asking you," his Grandma said.

Winking at the boy, the old man said, "Fries will be fine."

He turned to look as a pickup stopped at the gas pump and a rancher got out.

"It's just Jim," Whitey said. "He probably won't even come in till he comes back from town this afternoon."

The woman nodded and apologized - "Breakfast will be awhile. . . till I learn this kitchen."

As Whitey slowly got off his stool, she said, "I'm looking for stuff to put in the omelets. Is this meat beef?"

He looked at her. "Yup, of course it is. This is cattle country. . . . What'd you expect?"

"Oh, I don't know," she said. "Thought it might be wild jackass."

A few minutes later, the rancher walked in and said, "Whitey, that must a been some joke – I heard you way out at my truck."

* * * * *

As the old man and Joe came inside, Whitey announced to Sparkle, "Well, the tire's on, and we topped off the fluids. Other than that, everything's fine with the car."

The woman nodded and asked, "Do you two want anything?"

Joe got on a stool and said, "I'll have some rot-gut whiskey and a beer chaser."

His Grandma ignored him and looked at the old man.

"Maybe when I get back," Whitey said, as he headed for his apartment. The door marked Private was at the back of an alcove between the storeroom and a recess containing the mailboxes for the locals.

A pickup stopped on the gas-station side of the building, and a man wearing a long sleeved shirt, jeans and a wide-brimmed hat walked along the porch to the front door. As he entered, Sparkle smiled with satisfaction - he was wearing boots . . . an area-man who worked outside. Definitely not a tourist passing through.

The man, an Indian, stopped and searched the room with his eyes.

Sparkle asked, "May I help you?"

"I was looking for. . ."

Before he could finish, Whitey reentered the room. "Kid!" he exclaimed.

As they shook hands, the old man said, "God, Kid, you look beat. . . . Is everything all right?"

"Whitey, I need a place to sleep for a couple hours."

"Sure. Come on back."

Over his shoulder, he said to Sparkle, "I'll introduce you later. . . . We'll feed him then too."

Obviously, something more than lack of sleep was troubling the young man.

As soon as the two had disappeared into Whitey's apartment, a grizzled old bear of a man -another local - shuffled in, stopped to stare at the woman behind the counter and roared, "Who the hell are you?"

"I'm Sparkle," she said. "Do you want some coffee?"

"And I'm the gah-damn Lone Ranger . . . Make it strong and black."

As she poured a mug of coffee and he took a stool, she said, "You can't be the Lone Ranger."

"And why the hell can't I?"

"Cause you're alone . . . Unless you've got Tonto out pumping gas for you."

From his stool at the other end of the counter, Joe snickered.

Startled, the grizzled old bear glared at the boy and growled, "What the hell's going on here?"

No longer amused, the woman broke him off - "He's my grandson."

Sparkle moved around the counter to stand next to Joe facing the man.

They were in that position when Whitey came back. "Mack, I heard your bellow . . ."

He stopped and took in the scene. "What's going on here?"

The old bear turned to him and said, "You know how I talk, Whitey."

He turned back to Sparkle. "I'm sorry, Ma'am . . . I'm just a dumb Ol'fart who don't know how to talk to decent folk."

The woman slowly moved behind the counter again. "Okay . . . But Joe is who you should apologize to."

"Sorry, boy . . . Don't pay me no mind when I get to shooting my damn mouth off."

"I'll remember that," the young man assured him.

"Good," Whitey said. "Now, Mack, shut up, drink your coffee, and give me a twenty."

"Give you a twenty? . . . What the hell for?"

"The Kid's sleeping in back. His grandfather had some kinda stroke, and his grandmother is too weak to take care of him . . . They're having a blanket dance for 'em on the reservation . . . So give me a twenty for the blanket."

"Wouldn't it be cheaper if the Kid just sent some damn money 'stead of driving all that way?" But even as the old bear said it, he was reaching for his wallet.

"It's family," Whitey explained.

Then he looked at Sparkle and said, "You can see why our esteemed, retired deputy sheriff lives alone out in the back of nowhere - nobody can stand him, and he don't know people at all."

"That's about right," Mack admitted. "But I was a damn good deputy in my day."

* * * * *

The Kid eased his truck towards the blacktop and held his thermos out the window as a gesture of thanks to Sparkle. From the porch, she waved goodbye.

The other two waited until the Kid raised his now-empty hand in a high clenched-fist salute before they lifted their hands in response . . . All three watched till the accelerating pickup was well down the highway.

As they slowly returned to the lunch counter, Whitey said, "That was a nice lunch you packed for him. . . and that thermos of coffee."

Sparkle said, "I thought he could use some coffee on his drive home. He said it's another five or six hours . . . I'm glad Just Jim brought that grinder you wanted from town. He said you could pay him the next time he's in."

"Yup, I told him to get the best one they had, " Whitey said. . . . "Why'd you call him 'Just Jim'?"

"That's the way you introduced him."

"I did?"

"Yeah, you said, 'It's just Jim.' . . . So that's what I call him."

The old man chuckled and lifted his cup to her. "Good coffee," he said.

But, before he could finish his break, a car pulled up to the gas pump, and a woman got out of the passenger side to rush towards the store.

"Oh, hell," the old man muttered and headed for the front register. As soon as the woman opened the door, he said, "The key's right there . . . It's around the side."

Looking at his console and seeing that the driver who was pumping gas hadn't selected the "pay at the pump" option, he leaned on the counter to wait for her.

Meanwhile, Joe moved closer to Sparkle and softly said, "Grandma. . ."

Recognizing the look and the tone, she asked, "What is it?"

"I know the car's ready . . . But I don't think we'll be going for a few days."

She looked over her glasses and asked, "Are you telling? . . . Or asking?"

He squirmed a bit and said, "Just bringin' it up . . . Whitey showed me Eva's grave and wants me to put up the fence . . . He's already got the stuff and all. But it's just sitting there."

"What do you know about putting up a fence?"

"Oh, we'll do it together . . . He'll boss, and I'll do the grunt-work."

She paused before responding, "I guess it's settled then."

"You don't mind?"

"No, I don't mind. Not at all . . . But you should phone your dad so he won't worry about us being so late."

The boy nodded and asked, "Do you think Whitey will let me use his phone?"

"You'll have to ask him," she advised. "But first, as soon as those women leave, I want you to clean both rest rooms . . . Just 'cause you're fixing cars and building fence now doesn't mean you can forget your regular chores."

"Yes, Grandma."

She reached over and patted his cheek. "You're a good boy . . . You make your Grandma proud." He understood that she was talking about Eva's fence.

* * * * *

Sparkle and Whitey walked slowly away from the grave. After some thought, she asked, "Why's the sign going to say Eva's Place? . . . Since there'll be a a place for you beside her"

For awhile she didn't think he was going to respond. Then he said, "After I'm in the ground, won't nobody care what the sign says . . . Nope, this is Eva's Place."

They strolled in the twilight along the draw almost to the bridge for the highway.

The old man mused, "Those pancakes for supper were good."

"Everybody likes a good corn cake," Sparkle said with satisfaction.

Then she explained - "Lupe had some meal in the back of her truck when she brought the eggs. When I went out to get some potatoes, she had all kinds of good stuff. . . including the cornmeal."

"They got quite a co-op up in her village. . . mostly vegetables. Some fruit in season. Even wool and mutton, though they sell most of their sheep at the sale-barn in town. The eggs are from Lupe herself. I'm just one stop on her regular round."

After a pause he added, "That woman is one tough little cookie."

Sparkle looked at him. "Lupe? . . . I can see 'strong'. But tough? . . . She seems so gentle."

"Yup, she's gentle all right But tough too. About ten years ago, some rich guy bought the big ranch back that way and then tried to close off the only road to Lupe's village."

"How could he do that?"

"The road was on his land. He had title. . . claimed he had to close the road for liability purposes. . . Liability, hell. The guy just wanted to force those people outta the hills so he could have a bigger private hunting preserve to show off to his rich friends."

"But Lupe stopped him?"

"Yup, sure did . . . Rallied her people and a bunch of other folks too, including me and Eva. Got some Mexican and Indian lawyers to take the guy to court. They proved the village was there long before any Anglos got west of the Mississippi. Had some big-time professor read the original Spanish land grant to the judge. Of course, the judge ruled the road had to stay open and the owner couldn't do anything to hinder the use of it."

"Well, good for Lupe," Sparkle said.

"Yup. Then that guy tried to make a 'protect the fragile environment' claim on TV. But Lupe jumped on him hard. . . right there on TV. She said her people were part of this environment and took care of it for hundreds of years. . . and now this rich guy from back east wanted to 'protect the environment' by forcing her people off their land."

"I bet that went over well," Sparkle suggested.

"It sure did with people around here. But that rich guy almost got laughed out of the state. We got no problem with genuine environmentalists, but we hate phonies preachin' about it."

"What about the ranch?"

"Somebody else - a real rancher - owns the place now."

As they turned to parallel the road back home, Whitey said, "You're good at listening to an old man talk. But I'd like to ask you a couple things."

"Sure, go ahead."

"First, what's your real name?"

"My real name is 'Sparkle' . . . But my Social Security card reads Henrika Jones."

"Henrika." The old man mulled the sound over his tongue.

She went on - "My mother's favorite grandfather was a Swede who happened to fall in love with a black woman. I don't know if they ever married, but they sure loved each other . . . Anyway, when I was born, they named me Henrika after him."

"What about 'Sparkle'?" he asked.

She laughed and said, "In elementary school, I got into too many fights being called 'Hen' or 'Hennie'. The principal once said I had a lot of spark. And I told him, 'Yeah, I'm Sparkle.' So, that's been my name ever since."

As they approached the porch, he asked, "Why are you here? . . . From what Joe said about the deli where you worked, I have to wonder why you'd leave a good paying job that you're good at in your hometown. . . to head west to who-knows-what."

She didn't answer till they got to the corner, where they found Joe waiting. He reported to the old man - "There were just two customers for gas and some cold pop. And when your big sign came on, I closed up like you said. When I saw you down by the bridge, I thought I'd wait to tell you before I go watch TV."

"Good," the old man said. "I'll close out the cash register when I go in to bed."

Joe yawned as he got up. "G'night then. See you in the morning."

He kissed Sparkle. "G'night, Grandma. I may be asleep by the time you come in."

"I won't be long," she assured him.

After the boy left and the others sat down, Sparkle said, "I been thinking about what you asked. Are you sure you want to hear about it?"

"Yup, I'm sure."

"You knows the hand sanitizer I make Joe use all the time. . . "

Whitey chuckled. "Me too now."

She continued - "I learned about that when I was at the hospital visiting a friend. Every time a nurse came in, they'd squirt a little of that stuff on their hands, and I learned it was better than scrubbing with soap and water. . . . I was at the hospital because the woman's family couldn't stand going there. But they could count on 'good old Sparkle'. All they had to do was ask. My niece and her husband on Friday night. . . watch the kids so she could get a break while they go dancing. Then not see 'em till after Sunday midnight . . . I finally got tired of everybody asking all the time."

"Yup," the old man said, to let her know he was listening.

"Then last year, it dawned on me that Joe was the only one who wasn't pulling at me for something. He may not be blood but he really is my grandson. When his mother died down in Arkansas, his father had to take the younger kids home so his mother and sister could help raise 'em. And Joe decided he had to go help his family. So he gave the owner his notice. And two days later I told him I was going along. Shocked hell out of everybody. But by then, I didn't care, which kinda shocked me . . . I'd ride with Joe to his father's place and then take the bus to San Diego. Stay with a friend till I get set up for myself. With what I do, I know I can get a job all right."

She laughed and said, "Imagine. . . a woman my age starting over completely."

"I can imagine that very easily," Whitey said. "Did the same thing about your age."

"You did?"

"Yup, after Korea, I never stayed any place more'n a couple months. I know now I had post traumatic stress syndrome from getting my kidney shot out. At least, that's what the VA doctors told me a few years ago when I went to have the good one checked. But back then, most of us Korea and WW2 vets who'd seen too much and fought too much didn't call it nothing. Some of us drank too much when we got back, or hit too many people. But I just moved on. . . . Till I stopped here about fifteen years ago."

"That's funny," Sparkle said.

"Funny?" the old man asked in surprise.

"Not your life since Korea. . . . I meant - it's funny you're here after moving around so much. And I'm here 'cause I stayed in one place too long and it got too crowded."

"Yup, I see what you mean. . . . It is sorta funny," he said.

She leaned back in her chair to take in the night sky. "And here we both are - Elbow Room," she said. . . . "Not a bad place to be."

* * * * *

The community picnic to celebrate the completion of the fence took place about two weeks later. . . on Saturday afternoon so the school kids could come too.

By then, Sparkle had decided to stay on . . . to bask in the elbow room, as she told Whitey. The old man, whose name on his driver's license read Rudolph Valentino White, felt obligated to warn her - "There's not much money. . . nothing like you made in Chicago."

Then he exhaled in relief when she replied, "Who said anything about money? I'm just being neighborly. . . till I feel like moving on."

After a moment, she added, "I never thought I'd ever say this - but I'm going to do what I want. . . and move on when I feel like it."

By the time the fence was finished, Sparkle had a best friend in Lupe and a guaranteed welcome from the people in the village. She also served a 'Killer Burrito' on the days Lupe was able to deliver fresh tortillas from the best cook in the co-op.

The hard part for Sparkle would be when Joe finally got back on the road. But she told him, "Sometimes life's not easy, but a grownup faces it anyway. Your dad needs you now . . . And I'll only be three or four hours away, if you need me."

Her grandson nodded solemnly and then brightened. "You're right, Grandma. In Illinois, two hundred miles seemed like a long way. But out here, it's nothin'."

She patted his cheek as she said, "And the road's straight . . . Down hill both ways."

At the start of the picnic, Sparkle watched for grizzled old Mack, who now drove to the café almost every morning for his 'strong and black' and an order of corn cakes with fried eggs. Sure enough, he arrived early and, as he shuffled towards her, she pointed a finger and firmly said, "Mack, there'll be women and kids here today. I don't want. . ." She let her warning hang in the pleasant early autumn sun.

He looked down and said, "I know. I won't shoot off my gah-damn mouth."

"You got it, Big Guy . . . Did you bring a folding chair like I told you?"

"In the back of my truck," he said meekly. "I'll get the. . . I'll get it."

She pointed to the east side of the garage. "Sit over there in the shade till the food is ready. It'll be awhile, but I'll bring you a plate."

"I can get my own damn food," the old bear growled.

A big propane-powered grill had been brought over by two of Just Jim's hands when they came to put up the awning. Beef brisket that had marinated over night was being slowly grilled, with the aid of some fruit-tree chips from the co-op.

A smooth running truck pulled in to park next to Mack's. Sparkle saw it was the Kid and rushed over to meet him. The greetings were warm and sincere.

"How's your grandfather?" Before he could respond, she said, "No, wait. Whitey's inside. Let's go find him so you don't have to tell your story twice."

The old man, who had recognized the truck, met them on the porch. After more greetings, he also asked, "How's your grandfather?"

The young man smiled at Sparkle before saying, "Not as bad as I feared. He'll be in a nursing home for physical rehab for about a month. But there was no damage to his mind or his speech. And we set it up so Grandmother can share his room. . . . So, everything considered, it could have been a lot worse. The doctor said it was a warning shot across the bow. That Grandfather had to change his . . . 'life-style'."

Whitey snorted, and the young man laughed. "After all these years, Grandfather finally has a 'life style'. I wonder if Grandmother does too . . . And why would that doctor use a navy term - 'shot across the bow' - with us high-desert Indians?"

Then the Kid grew somber. "It was after midnight when I came back through, so I didn't stop to tell you about Grandfather."

Sparkle assured him - "As long as he and your Grandmother are all right."

Whitey echoed her - "Yup. No problem. . . . If you woulda woke me up, I'd probably got mad."

The Kid knew that wasn't true but appreciated the old man's words anyway.

A bit later, Lupe arrived from the village leading a small caravan of pickups and slowly drove her covered-bed rig close to the serving tables under the awning. She called through the opened window, "I've got most of the food. . . . But tell the others not to drive up here. We don't want too much dust raised around these tables."

The Kid and Joe sprang to the task. . . Joe, at first, because the older man did and then more eagerly when he saw Rosa, Lupe's teenaged daughter, riding in the second truck. Whenever she looked at him over her shoulder and called him 'Jose', he thought that the name he was born with sounded pretty good.

Fortunately, one of the village grandfathers was seated next to the door, with Rosa between him and the driver. Thus, when Jose opened the door, it was for the old man. Of course, he had to hold it for the smiling girl too.

Just Jim parked his truck in the growing line.

After greeting Sparkle, he called a greeting to the men in the lengthening shade by the garage. Mack had been joined by several others, including the village elders who had their own folding chairs.

The gathering immediately concentrated on the *patron* of the largest ranch in the area. . . a big-man who flew his own plane and used a helicopter on his ranch.

A few minutes later, another truck from the ranch slowly drove along the west side of the garage to stop by the newly completed fence. The men in back hopped out and removed two stepladders.

Then, as Jim led the other men their way, the ranch hands carefully lifted a sign out and placed it on the ground. The sign was made of treated wood with the name EVA'S PLACE burned into it.

One of the men, the owner of a much smaller ranch than Jim's, marvelled at the sign - "That's like the wood they used to make the porch . . . She would have liked that."

Jim nodded and said, "We used an old branding iron to burn the name in, and the bolts should fit the holes in the top of the arch."

Although the gate was barely wide enough for a coffin, when Whitey's time came, the arch was designed so that, even with the sign up, a tall man in a hat wouldn't have to stoop to get in. Whitey, who had put up a "closed for community picnic" sign on the front door, came close and looked down at the sign. He was followed by Sparkle and the others. Mothers shushed their children.

Jim indicated one of the stepladders that had been placed and asked, "Whitey, do you want to do it?"

The old man reluctantly said, "No, I'm past that now . . . Kid, would you do it for me?"

"Honored," the young Indian said as he stepped forward.

The rancher suggested, "Joe, what about the other side?"

"Honored," the boy said as he stepped forward.

Within five minutes, the sign was securely in place, and the ladders removed. As everyone looked up in satisfaction, the woman who ran the protestant church services three Sundays out of four, till the circuit minister came around again, stepped forward as planned and offered a short, tasteful and carefully prepared prayer to dedicate the fence and the sign. The villagers and most of the ranch hands and their families crossed themselves at the end of the brief service.

As soon as it was over, Sparkle announced, "The food's ready."

And Lupe added, "You children remember - elders go first."

As the others moved slowly towards the serving tables, Mack shuffled back to his chair and waited for Sparkle to bring him a plate. When she did, he groused, "Took you long enough. . . . And I want another beer."

"You're welcome," she said. "The beer's right there." She pointed to a tub of water-cooled cans about ten feet from where he sat.

* * * * *

It was early twilight, and some people were still lingering over food and conversation. A young ranch-hand got a CD player with large speakers from one of the trucks and set up well away from the grownups.

As soon as the music started, the young people started drifting that way and automatically formed a dance circle.

Sparkle, Lupe and several other women relaxed at the end of a serving table that had been cleared. Just Jim strolled in their direction, and the women stopped visiting to focus on him.

"Thank you, ladies, for the food," he said. "I'm a beef-man, but I really enjoyed that pulled pork . . . Very tasty."

A woman who had ridden with Lupe smiled at the compliment.

Then the man asked Sparkle, "Do you mind if I sit awhile?"

"Please do," she said.

He pulled a chair close and sat down. The others gradually resumed their conversation.

Sparkle and Jim sat comfortably until their attention was drawn by laughter from the men, who had moved their chairs out of the shade into the fading sun. Whitey was telling one of his stories.

Just Jim said, "This wouldn't have happened in the old days."

"What wouldn't have happened?"

"People from the ranches having a picnic with the villagers."

Then he explained - "We still had a lot of young Anglo hands then. After a few beers, some would always want to get tough with the young guys from the village, or get too fresh with the girls. Either way, we'd have a fight. So . . . no picnics."

"What's different now?"

"The only Anglo working for me the last few years was in my helicopter crew in Nam. Since then, the last thing he would want is to have a fight with anyone."

Puzzled, Sparkle said, "I don't recall him getting any food."

"No, he wasn't here . . . This would be too much for him, so he just stayed home."

With the sun low on the horizon, a beautiful, mournful sound suddenly touched the air. An Indian flute . . . The Kid was facing the arch to Eva's Place. By the time his tribute-song ended, everyone was silent and listening in awe.

With the flute cradled gently in his left arm, the young Indian raised his right hand above his head and, a moment later, lowered it to touch the earth.

Just Jim whispered to Sparkle, "He's calling on Father Sky and Mother Earth to bless what he's doing."

Then, as the Kid slowly walked clockwise around the fence, "Taps" for Eva from his flute moved some of the listeners to tears. Timing his slow walk to end with the last note, he faced the arch again to thank Father Sky and Mother Earth once more.

Just Jim whispered more advice to Sparkle - "Be sure not to praise him for his flute playing. He was seeking a blessing for Eva's Place . . . Praise for him would take away from the blessing."

She nodded and whispered a question - "Why did he walk around the fence as he played 'Taps'?"

"For him, Eva's Place is now a sacred site . . . That's why he walked clockwise - the sacred 'direction of the sun', as it was called before we Anglos arrived with our clocks."

She patted his arm to say thanks for being her teacher and said, "I won't say anything to him . . .But it was God Almighty moving for me."

"Taps" also proved to be the benediction for the picnic.

The trucks were quickly packed and, before they left, most of the people came over to say goodbye to Sparkle and to shake Whitey's hand.

The last truck to leave was Lupe's. Rosa rode with her mother this time and begged for a few moments alone with Joe to say goodbye before the young man drove home the next day. "Maybe I'll never see Jose again," she pleaded.

* * * * *

The next morning, the Kid used "pay at the pump" when he filled his gas tank. That way, there would be no issue about it with the old man.

At the lunch counter, Joe finished his omelet and country fries with a sigh of pleasure.

Sparkle gave him a small bottle of hand sanitizer and said, "Put this in my cup holder where it's easy to reach . . . And use it."

"I will, Grandma."

Whitey said, "And don't forget - you've got a job here any time, if it turns out you're not needed that much at your dad's place. I'm not getting any younger and can really use you around here . . .We could get hooked up on the internet so you could take some college classes like the Kid does."

Joe nodded in agreement and said, "I found out his name is Hector. It don't feel right calling him Kid . . . So I'll call him 'Hec' from now on."

"Why not Uncle Hec?" Sparkle suggested.

The boy teased, "Would that make him your son, Grandma?"

"I could do worse."

Then she added - "Don't be tempted to move back here too fast because of Rosa. Make sure everything is okay with your dad first. . . Seeing her when you come for a visit will be often enough for awhile."

"I know, Grandma."

The old man said, "I could probably fix you up with a truck so you could get up to the village any time you want."

Sparkle looked at him and said, "It sounds like you're trying to bribe the boy."

"Maybe I am," Whitey confessed. "I could make a trade with Joe, and then you'd have something to drive yourself to town."

The woman smiled and said, "Now you're trying to bribe me."

The old man confessed again - "Maybe I am."

The smiling Kid came inside and said, "Sparkle, we've only got a four-hour drive ahead of us, and you packed enough food for four days."

Whitey joined the teasing - "This woman's response to everything is food. . . And if something bothers her, it's more food."

She ignored them and said, "You boys be careful driving, and stop when you eat those sandwiches."

"We will, Grandma. . . unless Uncle Hec drives too fast in the lead."

The Kid smiled approvingly on hearing his new name and said, "We'll take it easy, and I know a spot about half way there to take a break."

As they walked outside, Sparkle had one final piece of advice for Joe - "I'll leave my cellphone on, so call me as soon as you get there . . . Or any other time."

"I will, Grandma . . . You don't have to worry," he said and kissed her goodbye.

She held the hug a bit longer than usual.

As the Kid eased his pickup towards the highway, he lowered the window and pushed his clenched fist into the air. Letting out a war whoop, he accelerated smoothly down the highway.

A moment later, Joe imitated Uncle Hec's departure, with his clenched fist reaching for the sky.

The two on the porch watched until the car and the pickup disappeared.

* * * *

That evening, Sparkle and Whitey wore light jackets as they sat in the corner. They were content. Joe had phoned from his dad's place, and Eva's grave was safe from wild jackasses.

The old man suggested, "Maybe we should get one of those electric things that look like a fireplace . . . Then when it gets too cold out here, we could fix up a corner in my place."

"Sounds good to me," she said.

After some congenial silence, she said, "That Kid can really play the flute."

The old man remembered and said, "Yup . . . Those months he worked for me, I'd open the window so I could hear it. He played most nights . . . I never told him . . . That was about a year after Eva died."

"Maybe he'll play for you. . . the way he did for Eva."

"It won't matter then . . . I'll be dead."

The woman protested, "Of course, it will matter."

Then she promised, "You'll be buried next to Eva, and the Kid will play his flute for you . . . I'll see to it."

Pleased, he asked, "You'd do that for me?"

"Sure would," she said truthfully . . . "Just being neighborly."

Chapter Fourteen (Tradecraft)
The spring of 1986, Istanbul

by Bob Shacochis

Her father flew in from Ankara to spend the weekend with her but this trip was special, his second visit in April, and tonight she would be having dinner with him, but where was the question, always the question, his habitat of mystery, his idea of fun, turning simple things into a challenge and a challenge into something simple. She knew only that their rendezvous involved, as always, a well-known and practiced game between them ever since she was a child in Kenya, yet this late afternoon as she left her school in Uskudar and took the ferry across the choppy, breeze-swept Bosphorus, the game had become for her a source of increasing ambivalence, if not outright exasperation, here on the occasion of her sixteenth birthday. She was in a hurry, or rather a state of hurriedness, her body tense with teenage urgency, already anxious to turn around and ride the ferry back to Asia, where her friends would be waiting for her in a coffeehouse on Baghdad Street. But, as always, there was no denying her father, although tonight, *her* night, she had promised herself to leave him no matter how much he begged her, *his heart of hearts*, *his darling Dottie*, to stay and walk arm in arm to mass at St. Basil's in the morning.

And now here was Europe and the busy mouth of the Golden Horn-*Hello Europe!* she sang to herself, reciting the mantra she had composed to express her utter joyous wonder with the magnitude of this city and the delicious fumes of its landings, brine and diesel and grilled meat and jasmine, *Asia begins, Europe ends, turn around, Asia ends, Europe begins, begin again, end again*¬--the ship rumbling as the captain reversed engines and the ferry nudged against the quay of Eminonu and the crew threw out the heavy ropes to men with outstretched arms, seagulls shrieking and the gangplank rattling into place, and she pressed into the crowd of dour Istanbullus streaming ashore with the by now familiar exhilaration of having so easily crossed continents, ignoring the hateful stares she had grown accustomed to from some of the men, although sometimes she would stare back brazenly at the boys her age, defying their clucking tongues and vulgar gestures, and wondered what, on this most important occasion of her life, her present might be, thinking she should have just come right out and told him her world would be more than perfect if she owned a Vespa. But the bus system is excellent, he'd say. Or, Take a dolmus. Her mother would just say scooters are suicidal, why not jump off a bridge, but that wasn't what her father would ever say.

She was to approach the donar kebab vendor on the east side of the termi-nal but, preoccupied with her post-dinner, après-daddy plans, she forgot what she was to ask him and had to dig her father's note from her shoulderbag and read the instruction again: His name is Mehmet. *Mehmet is a man who can see the future. Give him fifty lira and ask him for your fortune.* This Mehmet, like most Mehmets, was very happy to make her acquaintance. With the same hand he slipped her money into his windbreaker he withdrew a deck of cards, fanned them in his two hands, said pick three, and laid them out on the cutting block of his kebab wagon, pointing at one card and then the next. They were not the tarot cards she had expected, their faces printed instead with calligraphy, which she could not yet read although she was becoming rather good with Arabic in its Latinate form.

Ah, he said, squeezing her right hand in both of his and raising it in the air. Happy birthday. Happy happy. Allah sends you as his bright angel to this earth.

Far out, she said in English, as if she were one of the old hippies passing through the Pudding Shop on their way to Kathmandu; as if it were nineteensev-enty and she was traveling to India with the Rock and Roll Raj; as if she were her clueless, ex-flower child peacenik-turned-astronomically uptight mother.

This card, number two, said Mehmet. This card says you will leave here and go to the Cicek Pasaji to the place called Karaca and speak with a man who plays the violin.

Yes, okay, she said hopefully, finding her pen and scribbling in the margins of her father's note-*Flower Passage, violin*, and the name of the restaurant. Maybe tonight there would be no more to the game than this, dinner and the Flower Passage and then back on the ferry, but it never paid to underestimate her father's addiction to trickery and practical jokes and object lessons meant to be eye-open-ing. Mehmet lifted his chin toward something behind her and she looked over her shoulder to see a silver-haired man with eyeglasses, professorial in his tweed coat and baggy trousers, v-neck sweater and necktie, standing next to his Mercedes Benz, waving hello.

And Number Three? she asked.

Number three, he said, studying the remaining card and turning it face-down with a frown. Number three says you will have a prosperous life.

No it doesn't, she said. What does it really say?

You are clever, little sister. It says nothing.

Mehmet, are you really a fortune teller? she said, cocking her hip, resting her hands there, posing, not thinking she was flirting with him but she was. I'm sure my father told you what to say for two cards but not for three. What does the third one say?

It lies, miss, Mehmet said. It says what is untrue. It says you are my enemy.

That's crazy, she said with shocked laughter, lifting up on her toes for emphasis. Why would we be enemies? I love everybody in the world. Love, love, love.

It is a mistake, miss, said Mehmet. I am very sorry.

Sometimes these people enlisted by her father into the game worked for him in a capacity she no longer bothered to imagine, and he seemed to have access to an endless supply of them from all walks of life, businessmen, scholars, tradesmen, tough guys, police, bureaucrats, vagabonds. Sometimes they were simply people he had met on the street, at a newsstand or tobacco kiosk, in the library or a barbershop or café, and charmed into service. And who could resist a man so genteel and sunnily handsome and affable, a textbook case of the charismatic diplomat *circa* Camelot and American goodwill, well-groomed and dressed in Italian suits and always smiling, always a spark of sincere curiosity in his grey-blue eyes, or the twinkle of mischief that made people relax and laugh with him and feel free to say anything and want to do him a favor, what's the harm, he's a great man, surely you can see. She did not look like her mother, thank God, she looked exactly like him, but as she slid into the back seat of the sedan that had been waiting for her, munching the kebab Mehmet, with a lugubrious air of apology, had insisted she take, she thought that maybe the game was something she was now too young for or too old, depending on what she was trying to understand. The game had a life of its own of course, full of curious surprise, but by her father's design it evolved in unpredictable and obtuse ways and throughout the past year she had noticed the game change in a pattern that made her think he meant it to be something else than what she understood its intent to be, more to his purpose than to hers or theirs, less entertaining, less of a lark, more serious in tone perhaps, fashioned toward a different kind of education than the one he had determined to give her–it was hard to say, but then she had certainly sensed a similar shift away from clarity with all the boys she was coming to meet and find interesting in the bistros and lycees and colleges.

The game had started in Nairobi, her favorite place on earth before Istanbul, when she was ten years old. *I'm going to turn you into a flaneur*, he said, making her look up the word in the dictionary. Why he chose her for this project and not her brother was a moot point. The first time they played, what she privately liked most about it–that it was their game, no one else's--never seemed diluted but instead only enhanced by all the strange and marvelous characters her father led her too, and when she finally tracked him down, they would sit at a table in a side-walk café and she would sip her soda and eat her french fries or plantain chips or noodles and he would drink his glass of beer and they would talk animatedly and with loud disbelief or hushed admiration about this one or that one, the man who, the woman who, etcetera. Was he really a chief back in his village? Did you see her scars! Do you think that old man really was a sorcerer! Did that guy really kill a lion with just a spear! How do you know them, she asked, and he said they're friends of mine, and she said with awe, Dad, you're friends with *everybody!* As they took a taxi back to the new American Compound in one of the residential areas of the changing, modernizing city about to be transformed by Big Man politics, he leaned over to whisper in her ear, *this is our secret, let's keep it to ourselves, we'll say we went to the zoo*, a ruse which seemed only natural because she was already in the habit of keeping secrets and like most children understood instinctively how to protect herself with lies and omissions.

Quickly, the stage expanded from its original four blocks downtown to eight blocks and then doubled again, her knowledge of the once-intimidating city and comfort with its people growing accordingly, but then one day–by now she had turned eleven–he sent her off on the hunt into the squatter settlement known as Mathari Valley, where people were too friendly and clinging or not friendly at all, and she was intelligent enough to be amazed and angry that her father would let her wander unaccompanied through such dangerous quarters, but when that afternoon, trembling at the doorway of a bar thrown together walls and all from roof tin, peering into its sour, noisy darkness, she finally found him drinking beer with a throng of laborers, the place erupted with a cheer and the Africans were lovely, the men patting her on the head to run their rough hands across the golden silk of her hair, praising her bravery, giving her small presents of beads and marbles and all the roasted groundnuts she could eat, the singer among them making up a song in her honor, and she had never felt so marvelous or capable and never more at home in the world. Remember, don't tell your mother, he said, hugging her onto his lap, letting her take a sip from his cold bottle of Tusker. She wouldn't understand our game.

She'd disapprove, said the eleven year old, sounding sophisticated and wise with insight.

She'd disapprove, agreed her father with mock-severity. You've certainly got that right.

But a little blonde haired American girl walking by herself through those poverty-stricken neighborhoods, talking to vendors, stepping into shops to receive the next installment of her father's instructions–*Go to the open air market three alleys south and one street west* (he had given her a compass on her birthday) *and speak to the man who sells monkey meat* (Oh, gross! she had thought, reading the note), stopping to ask directions in Swahili (which she called dog language, because the dogs would obey her in Swahili but not in English)–of course her mother found out in no time at all. One of the cooks who worked in the American compound had seen her, one of the off-duty drivers from the Embassy, one of the askaris-watchmen--on the way home to the room where he slept during the day with the other askaris who had immigrated to the city from the countryside. The next day when her mother heard the reports she was furious and she went to her brother's room to sit with him while their parents argued.

Are you out of your mind, letting a child just walk around alone through those filthy slums! What were you possibly thinking!

I want her to be independent and free, I want her to know she's an American and can go anywhere and do what she wants, within reason. I don't want her growing up to be afraid of anything.

Hearing this from her father made her feel guilty and embarrassed and she sat on the edge of her brother's bed and consoled him with her tales of the city, which he never once resented but seemed instead to appreciate and always kept her confidence. But she couldn't stop herself from pitying him his fate, not because he had been ill for two months with malaria, not because walking home from school one day he had been viciously attacked by a pack of wild dogs that came charging over a hillside, not because he'd rather go to the movies than go on a safari and take pictures of the animals or better still, learn to shoot the rifles, not because she had to personally save him from drowning in the waves the year before when their entire school went on a field trip to the Embassy's beach house in Mombass, not because he absolutely hated the martial arts class they were made to attend together, taught three nights a week by one of the hyperactive Marines, and not because he was his mother's son just as she was her father's daughter, her brother with her mother's darker hair and rounder nose and soft shoulders and weaker chin but because she knew that her brother, three years older, had indeed grown up afraid of everything, and was becoming the unmentioned disappoint-ment to her father that she could never allow herself to be.

But this was one of the huge and irreversible reasons why she loved her father, loved him beyond tears though not beyond torment, because she had never heard him once express regret over having spawned a wimpish son, never heard a word of criticism directed at her brother's caution or self-absorption or shy reluctance to get with the team different than what was sent her way-*clean up your room, finish your dinner, homework, homework*--had never seen him humiliate her brother, had only witnessed her father's profound caring and affection and his unqualified encouragement that her brother find his own path, however timidly, through the hazards of the world, her father standing guard over them all.

She's eleven years old, for God's sake! There are people and things she needs to be afraid of.

I'd never place that child in harm's way and you know that. She was never in danger.

Then her father said something that illuminated the sensation she had felt at times during the game, when she had stopped at a crossroads and looked around, trying to get her bearing, that someone was following her. Later that evening when he was alone in his study she had asked her father about it and he said, yes, now next time I want you to see if you can lose him, and he bet her a dollar that she couldn't; she lost four before winning four, and then that part of the game seemed finished.

And if she gets any more independent you might as well plant a flag on the kid and declare her a sovereign nation.

There you go again, blowing things out of proportion.

In Africa, it had become clear to her that her father would allow her to accept no limits, and encouraged her in the rich extravagance of her lies, freedoms to which she responded with wilderness, a control her mother relinquished with only cursory resistance. At that age she did not know the word irony or its concept but she sensed its opposing realities nevertheless, experiencing the vague feeling that it must be difficult for a person like her mother to have a child as willful and unaccepting of boundaries as her daughter had proved to be, but for as long as she could remember, she had neither her mother's attention nor yielding affection. She was of course daddy's girl, but then so was her mother.

When she was younger she loved hearing the story about how her father, the young consulate in Morocco on his first foreign service assignment, had rescued her mother, a twenty-two-year-old Peace Corps volunteer raised in Fulton, Missouri, from imminent injury and perhaps a thousand deaths at the claw-like hands of tribal heathens massing outside the mud-walled house where she lived with a family of eight in a backroom without windows and ventilation and just a squat-hole in the yard for a toilet and was served her breakfast of bread and sheese and yogurt and her dinner of cous-cous and cauliflower by a silent wife watched over by an ever-changing number of teenage boys who, when the mother wasn't looking, rubbed their groins when she made eye contact with them, this disgusting tableau provided audio by the cackles emitted from behind the head to toe blue robes of an ancient grandmother planted for all eternity on her cushions in the corner of the kerosene-smelly kitchen, heathens who in truth were no more of a threat than can be posed by a well-behaved, overly disciplined room of doe-eyed Berber schoolchildren six days a week who mechanically repeated every syllable and package of English that left her mouth, including, after just two months in country, the declaration, *I think I'm losing it*, and the eerie discomfort of a village whose aloofness and ingrained sense of distance would never be an adequate measure of the gratitude it felt for the sacrifice of this young woman from John Kennedy's America, to leave her home and cross the earth for the sake of the future of its children. No matter, the shock of the North African culture invaded her mother's system as a form of mental paralysis.

Her father, it was well-known throughout the expatriate community in Morocco, exercised an open door, open phone policy at his villa for any volunteer in from the countryside for r&r or medical treatment or whatever (meaning hopping in the sack with westerners), plus use of his chlorine-saturated swimming pool and the twenty-four hour attention of his three domestics (they came with the lease and there was no getting rid of them). On the day he returned home from the consulate to find his living quarters filled with the panting sobs of an attractive young and to his eye extraordinarily sexy midwestern girl in the throes of a nervous breakdown, he ordered his housemaid to soothe her with an almond oil massage and his houseboy to supply food, drink, and, should she want it, a pipe of hashish (she wanted it, but being stoned only magnified her distress), then walked down to the city center and had his supper watered with several round of gin and tonics and walked back up the cobbled streets to the villa to find the volunteer on the phone in his study, hyperventilating transatlantically to her parents in Missouri, and he took the phone from her grip and spoke calming, reassuring words to her family and replaced the receiver in its cradle and said what can we do to make you feel better and she said she wanted to go to church, and he said do you want to wash up first and she nodded tearfully and it took the rest of the night for her to scrub herself free of the germs of hysteria and disorientation but by Sunday dawn they were side by side in a pew and St. Eusti's, celebrating first mass, sharing the immediately profound bond of their Roman Catholicism. And by noon they had changed into bathing suits to retire poolside for a service of tea and fruit, and then later that afternoon, with the servants told to get lost, in the pool, naked but, even so, circumspect. By twilight her father to be had discovered what her mother to be most needed, which was to be held in the tender arms of the familiar.

That was how the story of her mother began, she thought, noticing that the driver had begun to circle the Hagia Sophia a second time, and only God could say how it would end, though the ending already seemed to have taken place some time ago. You could not conceivably pack more irony into a life than had been stuffed into her mother's, a woman who desperately wanted to escape the terrifying exoticism of what was not the world she had been born to inherit and yet had guaranteed her exile from it by falling in love with the one person who would not only keep her from returning home but render the destination of home itself permanently temporary and therefore impossible. And how could her mother ever live in the States again, her daughter thought unkindly, without her legion of servants, without the accumulated privileges of the status that only came from living overseas and nowhere else, the viceroy's wife.

They had married one had to think too hastily in Casablanca, her father undoubtedly expecting her to be the virgin that she was, her mother having never given procreation a thought, except to do anything with boys that caused them, in their constant but easily assuaged desire, to fall short of their goal. Then he surprised her on their honeymoon in Paris by leaving her there in a walk-up apartment on the Left Bank, a war bride and freshly pregnant, and flying away to his new assignment in Saigon. She liked Paris but despaired of being left alone, found the student riots thrilling but almost everyone she tried to talk to was an insufferable snob (she didn't have to mention she had a husband in Vietnam to be blamed for the war), and often she forgot that she was pregnant and imagined instead that she had contracted some awful African disease. After her brother was born, her father visited his new family like clockwork for ten days every other month for a year, then three months in, three months out for an entire second year and then she reclaimed him full-time, starting with his recovery from a bullet he had taken to his left shoulder during the Tet offensive and then eleven months back in the States in the suburbs of Washington DC (where her father purchased one of the new townhouses mushrooming through the fields of Vienna, Virginia), followed by two years in New Delhi, where their daughter was born, her mother's bad sense of humor sticking her with the name she would come to abhor, Dorothy, as if to punish them both for not being somewhere else where they belonged, sinking soon afterwards into a post-partum depression, withdrawing to a room she took as her own at one end of the sprawling house where she simply lived in bed all day, listening to American folk music and smoking vast quantities of pot out of a chillum and when she finally emerged she had, in her husband's words, *gone hindu*, wearing saris, visiting gurus, making a pilgrimage to the Ganges and returning to an infant and a small boy who seemed, perplexingly, as much a part of the house as the servants and rented furniture and peacocks in the yard and just as removed from her sense of responsibility, which continued to resist definition, her brother remembering the amas and nannies and sometimes their father changing diapers and dressing them but never their mother.

Cairo, her mother was vindictively fond of saying in the years ahead, made her come to her senses, her husband's reassignment to North Africa more than she could bear–she might pretend to *go hindu* but she'd never go *muslim*--and for the one and only time she fled, not just back to America but all the way back to her parents' cozy red-brick bungalow on a quiet maple-lined street in Fulton, her alcoholic but good-natured father an agricultural extension officer for the university in Columbia, her book-loving but narrow-minded mother tenured at

Westminster College, and she listened to their cautious admonitions, their unplacating concerns–*but honey this is the life you've made; I would think an annulment is not something the Vatican makes easy*-and answered always with two minds, self-doubt the only common trait between the pair–*But you don't know the things he does*, she'd say direly, unable or unwilling to explain, and then in the next breath, *He's the most altruistic, dedicated man. I know you'll just love him to death*, and then she'd wedge in a half-formed unconvincing diatribe on American imperialism that would cause her parents to shake their heads at her naivete. She had arrived in Missouri thoroughly exhausted and at the end of her wits, international travel with two small children clearly a message from God that God hates you. Finally though she started to refocus on her children, those adorable but neglected creatures, as something other than a curse without remedy, seeing them bounced on their grandfather's knee or clutched giggling and squirming to their grandmother's bosom, reminding herself she had to somehow relax about the whole idea of motherhood; *think of the children*, her mother would tell her quietly as they stood at the kitchen, washing up after meals. *But that's what I've been trying to tell you*, she'd say back in a rebuke to her own mother, who, not having walked in her shoes, understood nothing about her situation. *These places we have to live, they're no place to raise children. It's not the poverty. Poverty doesn't have to be so dirty, does it? It's their attitude about things.*

For instance, said her grandmother, although she had no tolerance herself for uncleanliness.

Women, said her mother. *The men treat the women worse than any stray dogs.*

Well fine, said her grandmother to her mother. There were plenty of decent folks right here in Boone County who needed a helping hand. Why go traipsing off to Timbuktu to make yourself useful? Well, I'm not blind, her mother said to her grandmother, but there was nobody in America except maybe Negroes who were as bad off as the people out there in the muddle, but she had felt called, as a freshman at Wash U. watching the television when JFK, campaigning in Michigan, had spoken directly to her, telling her if he were president he would create and agency for young people just like her, bursting with unshaped idealism but ready to help bit by bit make the world better, and then he was president asking what she could do for her country, but she hadn't been called to help American Negroes or poor white trash in the Ozarks and didn't want to anyway. Now here she was, knowing the call was a mistake, crossed wires, and she felt her life had been misassigned and she was doomed to be forever remorseful that she had not succeeded in her callow passion to make a better world, or make even one life easier; instead, she had made her own worse.

Revision

by Richard Jones

I choose to believe, that on holiday from foggy London with their daughter by the sea in the south of France, and without the remotest conception that a committee of translators had long been working to bring into submission the many errors of the King James Bible, "the noblest monument of English prose," my mother and father were inspired to conceive a child on September 30, 1952, unknowingly celebrating—as farmers harvested hillside vineyards—the publication in America of the translators' Revised Standard Version, which was later revised and published as the New Revised Standard Version, a model of accuracy, clarity, and euphony that might define a poet's aesthetic, a red pew Bible whose depths their grown son, born three weeks late, would one day plumb with prayers for illumination.

Train To Szczecin

by Kenneth Pobo

Passing through the north
German countryside, often
I wonder if I'm in Wisconsin—
Stan and I on folding chairs
watching herons. Several

men drink sangria. One
wobbles toward the bathroom.
Another throws an empty
out of the window. After
the blond German passport guy
checks us out, I stretch, bury
my head in a book.
In Poland,

another passport guy checks
name, birthdate. I remember
gay Germans herded into trains
with Jews, dark Gypsies,
anyone un-Aryan.

The passport men with gold
wedding rings, an engineer
who drives but is never seen--
we enter new places
knowing nobody or how

to get around. Sometimes
there is no getting around.
Doors open. They put you
where they want you.

The Heights of Ollantaytambo

by John Lane

For Thomas Pierce

I.

Rio Urubamba carves the Sacred Valley north, brown current kicking up, bound for Amazonia, 500 miles distant. We climb quickly, ahead of tour tourists, who came in combies.

The Incas saw mountains as holy–these high ruins, stacked stones dragged from a distant quarry and shaped on the side of a hanging Andean valley.

We try to see through time and tourists, to moments when this alter was more than a photo prop.

How hard not to look down on today's town and the red-shirted Peruvian guide in a blue baseball hat.

Her English is stilted but steady as she explains to one gray-haired patron how the Incas worked smooth angles by improvising coca spit and gravel.

From the valley rises the strands of Bob Marley's "Stir it up" -- a voice from this time, not theirs.

II.

Mancha Inca rigged the plain below

with channels to route Spanish conquistadors, their horses mired in flood water.

The Spanish retreated to Cuzco, leaving the Inca a few years of freedom still– but now tourist busses crowd the lowlands once trouble for Pizarro's legions.

White men climb Mancho's steps to rent his view.

They say time moves in circles up here,

that stones and sky speak one tongue

unknown to those who listen to tour guides, but some things never change– the sun declines west and the valley now fills with Bob Marley's "Redemption Song" drowning the tourist train to Aguas Calientes.

III.

A black dragon fly jerks past, pushed by wind from the distant valley floor. Yellow flowers used for dye bloom in the ruin's cracks.

Honey bees work an abandoned plastic bottle of Inka Kola. Mustard colored lichen spreads on the pink inca stone alters. Sometimes the stone steps forward-- they built in the mountain, not on it.

I think of Neruda and his love for small ordinary things- native rock, the women weaving as they walk, how he found strength in these short residencies on earth. He wrote about a gift of socks, or even the abandoned mystery of Machu Pichu, 30 miles north.
Like Neruda we too will descend from these heights, but always carry Ollantaytambo in the space left in our low land blood where oxygen used to flow. If these stones hold memory, then what's left for us to know?

Here
Philip Dacey

There is no point. It happened, and we're here.
What's missing can be made up as you go.
The point is fiction in a living ear.

That stars were dice and threw themselves is clear.
Imagine arms of fire, pips aglow.
How could there be a point? It happened; we're here.

You've won the lottery. Now give a cheer.
The ones who lose don't have a chance to know who's won, who's lost, or fiction
in an ear.

To think: you almost weren't! No wonder you're so dear.
I'm glad you're my companion for this show that has no point. It happened, and
we're here.

Randomness? Call it a rose to fix in your hair.
Tumbling through space, the numbers declare, "No point, no point," but
fictions soothe in the ear.

We do a kind of tap dance in the air
at a great height. Let's enjoy the vertigo since there's no point. It happened,
and we're here.
All points are fictions in a living ear.

Eating Illinois

by Dan Guillory

The tender parts, the haunch

And liver and sweetbreads,

Are the first to go.

Like counties, their over-cooked

Joints fall apart, meat tattered on the bone,

Smaller and smaller fragments, Shelby

From Crawford, Macon from Shelby

And from Macon itself, Moultrie and Piatt.

The lonely line of separation, the cord

Knotted from mother through sons

To fathers, stretches taut as a tow-line

A clean and legal demarcation

Like townships into counties.

We live as maps,

The menus of the earth.

And under it all the heart beats incessantly

While the river flows in a crooked black line

Even when covered with ice.

The Plymouth

by Richard Jones

In a corner of a field, at the edge of an old wood,
a tire-less automobile, abandoned in mud and weeds
to rust and crumble, befriended me the saddest year
of childhood. While my cousins walked to school,
I'd let the screen door slam behind me, and run
through town to the abandoned farm where,
doorless, the black car waited. I'd climb inside
and spin the speedometer's limp, drooping arrows,
imagining life's endless road unfolding, beckoning.
I could hear the engine roar and purr, waiting for me
to put the car in gear. I'd grip the big steering wheel
and drive somewhere exotic, like Sheboygan or
Green Bay. This was long ago, in Savannah,
where I'd never seen a snowflake or a frozen lake,
when the world was still a place to be imagined
rather than remembered, as I remembered it today,
when the caravan of classic cars rolled slowly past,
and I spotted my good old friend, the big-fendered
1940 Plymouth, proudly waxed and shining, piloted
by a grinning white-haired man in a blue sports cap
who waved as he passed, and looked just like me.

Molly's Bed

by Bonnie Jo Campbell

The creek running below Molly's bedroom window was full of ducks yakking about field corn and snapping turtles and about the days getting shorter, and the noise woke Molly from a dream about roto-tilling next year's garden. As the donkeys dragged a patch of soil, tomato and bean plants sprang up behind their hooves. In her waking life, Molly planted five acres of vegetables, the biggest garden around here, and she planned one way or another to keep on, even if she had to do it without the Ford tractor. This July, after thirty-five years of faithful service, the engine had finally blown. During the school year she worked as a junior high lunch lady, but the summer months were all for the garden. September and October were hellish busy, especially now with canning tomatoes, but there was no law saying a woman couldn't work hard.

"Damn noisy ducks," Molly said. "Get the hell out of here, fly off south, won't you?" She would miss those ducks when they disappeared in a few weeks, but from her ex-husband she'd gotten the habit of lying in bed cursing them this way, and she was a woman of habits.

"Dumb ducks," said another voice, quietly.

"What?" Molly sat up to make sure she was awake.

"Dumb ducks," said a man's voice.

"Is there some body in my bed?" Molly's bed was bigger than a king-sized, so big that they'd had to special order the mattress. Her ex-husband didn't think any smarter than filling the whole room with a bed. Molly was always having to keep her kids from jumping around on it.

"It's just me," said Wendell Wagner, who'd been repairing the furnace last night. Molly had debated long and hard about whether to spend money fixing the thing, knowing she might not be able to afford fuel oil this winter anyway. She ought to figure out how to heat with wood, but last night she had been cold and the kids'd been cold and so she'd called Wendell. He was good with an old oil burner, and he'd never overcharged her before, and ever since that fancy-dressed fool of a wife of his throwed him out, his advertisement at the hardware store said he was available any hour of the day or night.

Wendell said, "You told me I should stay the night if it got too late."

"You're supposed to be on the couch."

Molly's husband had taken off at the first whiff of spring a year and a half ago, and Molly had survived just fine without him. She'd planned to never lie down with one of them cheating, troubling sons of bitches again, but here she was lying with a fellow in the very bed her husband had built. He'd built it from some particular live oak wood, and for some reason got the idea of hitting the headboard with a chain to make it look old, and then shellacked it specially. It wasn't three months after he'd finished the monstrosity that he left town. Molly wondered if he'd built a bed for the gal at the bottle gas company too.

Molly said, "I put a quilt and a blanket out there on the couch for you."

"I must've walked in my sleep," Wendell said. "Or maybe that big yellow dog was lying on the couch." In fact, Wendell had followed the sound of Molly's snoring to find her bedroom, and he had climbed into the enormous bed quietly so as not to disturb her, and he'd stayed way over by the far edge. Wendell would never have dared climb into a regular bed with a woman, but he figured that in a bed this big maybe she'd get used to him before she even noticed him.

"You better not be naked," Molly said.

"I don't think I am." Wendell lifted the blanket. "Nope, I'm not naked."

"Good thing. 'Cause if my kids had come in here and found you naked, they'd do terrible things to you."

"What kind of terrible things?"

"Oh, one fellow who crawled in my bed, they stole his trousers and filled them up with stinging nettles. The way he howled when he was putting on those pants, you'd a thought cannibals were cooking him.

"I still got on my trousers," Wendell said. "My shirt too. Is that a true story you're telling me?"

"Another sleepyhead fool, they drug him out and hooked him between my two donkeys," Molly said. "Those donkeys pulled on him till he got to be a very tall man."

"I'm already over six foot." Wendell turned toward Molly in the bed, smiling as much as he dared. "Do you prefer a tall man, Molly?"

"No reason you should care what I prefer," Molly said lacing her fingers over her stomach, glancing over at Wagner, whose face and body was dappled with sunlight.

Molly's husband had been a very tall man, six foot six, which he gave as his reason for needing such a bed, though Molly had suspected he was just trying to sleep farther away from her. Though she hated his sneakiness, she didn't really blame him for leaving—they hadn't had much in common besides the kids. He'd wanted her to sell this old place, build a new house, travel around the country even. He'd gotten tired of a woman who wanted to garden all summer. When he left town he left the gal from the bottle gas company behind too, which showed he was looking for something entirely new.

A dog barked outside. Chickens crowed in the chicken yard. The dog paused for the crowing, then barked again.

Molly said, "But since you asked, I prefer a man who's not a lying cheating sneaking son of a bitch."

"Should I get up and let the dog in?" Wendell said.

"Oh, the kids'll let him in."

"You think I ought to go out the window?" Wendell said. "So your kids don't see me?"

Molly paused to think. "No, you'd better not. If you go out the window you'll make them ducks crazy, wake everybody."

"I hear somebody yelling in your kitchen," Wendell said, "Sounds like your kids might be fighting."

"That's just how they eat breakfast. My husband used to holler at them but I don't mind a little back and forth. Gets the blood moving. Warms a person, even." In fact, as recently as yesterday morning she'd yelled for them to shut up, but really that was just a way she could join into their conversation.

"Listen to them donkeys he-honking in the barnyard." Wendell said. "They do that every morning?"

"They figure I ought to be out feeding them instead of lying here talking to you," Molly said. "Why aren't you sleeping at your own place, Wendell?"

"It's too quiet at my apartment. Never could relax with quiet. Though I do appreciate a smooth-running oil burner. Listen now." Wendell turned his ear toward the vent near the foot of the bed. "Do you hear that furnace kick on? Smooth as glass."

They both listened for a moment.

"That's smooth all right," she said.

"And you don't smell any fuel do you?"

"No telling when the thing's going to break down again," Molly said.

"My work's guaranteed," he said. "You can call me if it breaks down, any hour of the day or night. And maybe I can take a look at that old Ford tractor you said's got a blowed engine."

"You know I can't afford to pay you to fix my tractor."

"Maybe I'll do it in my spare time," he said. "If you don't mind it taking a while, and then in the summer you could give me some tomatoes." Wendell could imagine working for a few hours between furnace jobs, then taking a break to drink some coffee with Molly as he studied the Ford manual he'd have borrowed from Joe at the hardware store. He wondered if Molly would ever drink coffee in bed. Or eat in bed, or play gin rummy here.

"Why'd your wife kick you out, Wendell?" Molly asked.

"Claimed she couldn't stand my snoring any more. For the last two years she made me sleep on the couch. Then one day she said she couldn't stand to look me any more.

"Well, I didn't hear you snoring," Molly said. "And I never liked quiet anyway."

"Quiet is lonely, if you ask me," Wendell said.

Molly didn't know if Wendell had any more idea than she did about the business of overhauling a tractor engine. There was no law, though, said she couldn't give a man a chance.

A language has many parts

by E. Ethelbert Miller

He realized there were many parts of her he liked
She reminded him there were many parts of her – he didn't know
He wanted to be inside her
She said she was not empty
(Conversations are only between cities)
He went to bed wondering if he would catch the train before daybreak
She found his hand between her legs
He left his hat in her apartment
She decided to fuck him now that he was gone
He thought it was rain on his fingers – it was her
She liked the smell of the trees and her river
He was drowning when the train crossed the bridge
She looked at the window and heard a whistle blowing
He missed the train and headed back to where she lived
She realized there were many parts of him she liked
He reminded her there was one part of him – she didn't know

The Graduate Student's Wife

by Alice Mattison

I'd been married to the man for decades, but he surprised me. In his fifties, Edward did not lust after a boat, a farm, or a girlfriend. He wanted to go to graduate school.

Edward never liked school. I should know. I was his girlfriend in junior high, and again– after a long gap– when he was in law school. He treated both the same way: arguing with teachers, finding reasons not to do homework. He cared about politics and poor people, and had been a legal aid lawyer or someone a lot like a legal aid lawyer since earning his law degree. Now, he said, he wanted to listen to thoughts other than his own. And the way to do this was to go to the Kennedy School at Harvard, which had a "mid-career" master's program.

He seemed to assume that if he simply waved his hand, I'd follow him (along with our geriatric dogs, a German Shepherd and a gray terrier). I'm a novelist. "You can scribble anywhere," Edward said. I also teach, but it's in a low-residency master's program, which means that for three weeks a year I live at Bennington College, and the rest of the time I receive mailed packets of work from student writers. There was no reason they couldn't mail their stories to an apartment in Massachusetts instead of our house in New Haven, Connecticut.

Yet I resisted. We'd lived in the same house for more than twenty years, a tiny house built for factory workers in 1874; we'd reared our three sons– now grown– there. I let the dogs out and in a dozen times in an afternoon without losing my train of thought. I did favors for my aged and frail parents– who lived a mile away– without ruining my week. My imagination stretched lazily during long solitary days in the presence of familiar pictures and objects.

I tried to picture us moving into an apartment near Harvard. Our kids would help carry furniture and boxes, and neighbors would see a nice middle-aged couple, apparently assisting their graduate student children. At the end of the day, though, the graying parents would stand waving on the front steps, while the children drove off, calling, "Study hard!"

It didn't seem right. It didn't seem possible. Who would look after my parents? What apartment would take two dogs? And– since it became clear that I'd have to come home often to see my mother and father– what precisely would we be carrying in?

"What about furniture?" I asked.

"Furniture?" he said.

I complained to friend after friend, until one said her parents' furniture was stacked in her basement. When the time came, we rented a U-haul truck, drove to her house in Vermont, loaded a bed and other necessities, and drove to the only apartment that took dogs in Somerville, Massachusetts. We arrived after dark and– my fantasies notwithstanding – alone. The kids were coming the next day with our car and the dogs. We parked the truck in the only empty space on the narrow, hilly street– in somebody's driveway. She came out and explained that we'd have to move in an hour so she could drive the baby-sitter home. We dragged my friend's parents' furniture and our boxes of laptops and clothes and dishes and pots into the apartment. Then we drove around Somerville until, miraculously, we found a place where we could legally park the truck overnight. Then we hiked until we found a restaurant still open at 10:30 at night and, our middle-aged bodies sagging with exhaustion, ate our supper.

I began my routine. On alternate Monday mornings, I'd secure a laptop and a bag to a luggage cart with bungee cords. Watching, the German Shepherd would raise her snout and gaze in despair at the ceiling. I'd leave anyway– maybe kissing the dogs goodbye more fervently than I kissed Edward– walk down an endless hill and take the T to Boston, then Amtrak to New Haven, then the bus to my house, where the phone would be ringing as I put my key in the lock: my mother. "Are you coming today?" I'd walk up another hill to their house. I'd change their lightbulbs and cheer them up.

After I had alternated weeks in New Haven and Somerville for three months, an Amtrak clerk said something I didn't like and I burst into tears. I was ashamed not to be able to manage such a tame version of a commuter marriage– other couples we knew commuted between continents– but I couldn't. Yet when I took Amtrak back to Boston on Saturdays, I was glad. Edward met me as I emerged from the Porter Square T stop with my luggage cart and bungee cords. My boyfriend, my lover– he was the sexy young guy I stole away from home to visit. We had good weekends.

But during the weeks I spent with him, we fought. He was around. He talked. He expected things. Our nearly bare apartment was haunted, especially the back bedroom where I was expected to scribble. I didn't see anything, but I felt something. Edward was skeptical until we saw an ad for a nearby apartment. "Not Haunted," it began. Finally I moved my laptop into the living room and he started working in the back bedroom. He said, yes, there was a ghost– but he didn't mind it.

I posted rules on the refrigerator:
1.Rule of Solitude
Alice is to be left alone on weekdays from late morning to four p.m. unless she has agreed otherwise.

2. Rule of Acknowledgment

Any risk of interrupting Alice's writing hours should be acknowledged in words or gestures.

3. Rule of Lunch

On weekdays, each person is responsible for his or her lunch.

By spring, there were lovely hours: two of us writing at either end of the apartment. For the first time in his life, Edward did homework. One afternoon I heard him on the phone with our middle son, who'd just gotten a new job and had turned to his father for advice. Edward was saying that he'd be happy to help our son choose a retirement plan, but not just now— he had a paper due in an hour.

We gradually adjusted, but life— our real life; our middle-aged life— kept happening. My mother spent a few days in the hospital. Our sixteen-year-old terrier, Sally, died of kidney disease. Finally, my father broke his hip, and with complications spent seven weeks in the hospital and rehab. The remaining dog and I moved home. What a relief. Sometime later my aunt made a little speech about my sacrifices, her voice breaking. "It's not just that you help your parents," she said, "but— to be apart from your husband for seven weeks!" I didn't tell her that otherwise I might have strangled him in his sleep.

But we stayed married, and when my father was home and stable, we spent three weeks together in Somerville with our lone, sad dog. It was romantic— young love. And Edward— who'd learned a lot that year, one way or another— had a master's degree.

Holding On

by Anne Calcagno

S he observed her own aging with method. A woman's throat went first, pieces of skin loosening like tent flaps. Her neck that was once a column, became a slack stack of linens. Her jowls swayed. Then her hands swelled. Veins rose, now occasioned to announce their circuitry, and two once silky fronds became distorted. In particular, Kate disliked the purple etchings — sickly winter twigs! — that had tattooed themselves into piles of kindling on her thighs. Her adolescence *had* coincided with the mini skirt and her discovery of male thigh appreciation.

Kate noted every decline, depression, and deviation rationally. She wasn't going to wake up one day, look in the mirror, and practically have a stroke over what she'd refused to predict.

She taught writing part-time at a community college west of Chicago and Oak Park, Ernest Hemingway's home. Kate aimed to be a bodiless lesson, an instructive mouthpiece. It was hard enough to enthuse students over Composition 103, without throwing the teacher's decaying flesh into their confused calculations. They must learn sentence structure, noun-verb relations, thematic unity. *The subject is the word that tells what the sentence is about, she read aloud. A preposition can form a phrase of exclusion within the sentence.* Advocate of The Essay, Kate championed muscular paragraphs and deft rhetorical moves.

At the end of her day, on her forty-five minute commute home, she did not want to hear herself another second. She grew even more annoyed with the self-indulgent radio DJs. Talk, talk, talk, *ad nauseam*. Were there that many people out there, desperate to get anyone's blather? Kate rammed her thumb into the *power* button.

Driving, she daydreamed. She climbed into her past, compiling a list of her finest moments:

1) Rode Kawasaki motorcycle alone from Seattle to Chicago (1981)
2) Skinny-dipped twice in Lake Michigan with Ellen and Joan (1983)
3) Got pink cherub tattooed on left buttock (1985)
4) Posed nude for boyfriend, Jack, the B&W photographer (1987)
5) Rolled own joint, standing in the snow, on Mt. Hood (1988)
6) Earned Master's Degree in Modern American Literature, (inspired by Kerouac) (1991)
7) Quit the pot habit / Became devoted vegetarian (1992)

Time decomposed the familiar, but Kate owned what her body *had* done. So, the moments of triumph didn't last forever. Every day, every stupid commute, ended too.

A couple of weeks later, after class, lilac-scented spring air wafted pleasantly through the windows. One of her favorite students, a young moon-faced man named Mike had stayed to talk. He was struggling to improve his essay on "American Indifference to the Homeless," when Kate farted, loudly. Kate had been growing enthused about his ideas, his desire to convey the grave costs of societal negligence. She had been gesticulating with her hands, a trait inherited from her Italian mother, emphasizing his essay's potential, when her bottom exploded right from under her. An awful percussion. With natural graciousness Mike murmured: "Don't worry about it," and went on to ask about the body of his paper. She wanted to blurt: "That wasn't me!" But the two of them were alone in the classroom, tilting over his paper. If she could have melted away into oblivion in that moment, she would have.

She had quietly gauged each stumble into aging, but the culprit still managed to upend her. In fact, her moment of rectal degeneration had overcome her right when she most counted on herself. Mike was so concerned with the homeless that he hardly seemed to register her blushing mortification. Once, she *had* been a young woman who regularly lost her heart and mind over a smooth chest, a gravelly voice, a girl who would *never* have farted in the presence of a guy. Until she became this field cow.

Their conversation had seemed interminable. Later, she hadn't the faintest idea what she'd said about the narrative of his essay. Driving home, she almost cried. She should have laughed like a truck driver: hah! hah! hah! But she felt weepy. At home, she climbed into her nightgown, though it was only seven o'clock. She sank under her bedcovers. She reached for the TV remote control. Last year, as a promotion for the thriller *Bullet To Your Heart*, they'd done a mailing to customers of remotes shaped like guns. Moving channel to channel, Kate imagined blasting off every pretty model's head.

She woke up to bright daylight and an ABC news flash – one hour earlier, in South Carolina, a high school sophomore had opened fire with a semi-automatic on his denuded PE class. The footage showed bloodied bodies ricocheting against lockers or crumpled on the ground in BVDs. The kid had also blown his own brains out. His hunger for attention -- or respect? retribution? -- had been greater than the cry of *life*. What must it be like go around exploding the life out of people?

Her students, for the most part only one year out of high school, had to be reeling, confused. This should be the day's topic of discussion. They'd learn to curtail their shock by shaping it into clear-headed arguments. She created their assignment topic: "Youth Violence in America: Aberration or a Growing Disease?" She drove to Pine Woods Community College, thinking about which angles to raise, privately wondering if shooting sprees were becoming average fare. How would she know if a psycho was registered in her class until it was too late?

Kate stood in front of the blackboard, urging, "Writing marries logic and emotion, reason and rhetoric. The tragedy in South Carolina can be your central focus or only one of the examples you utilize. Take your ideas seriously, support them with research. Imagine that you are writing to effect change."

A hand shot up, "But no one else reads the essays."

A technicality; why was that their principal insight into argumentation? Their dependable request for the actual: *I'll think about change if you tell me who'll make it happen.* "That's not the point. You have to practice to play." They did not trust play-acting. "Your essay can *create* a determined reader. Write, and they will come!"

Someone laughed, "Yeah, right." At the approach of the second millenium, students trusted things more than ideas. What could she do?

Driving home, she pondered what tipped the scales to violence. Turning off the highway, nearing home, the traffic plodded. She glanced at the solitary faces, moving slowly parallel, locked behind steering wheels. All at once, she was struck by the possibility for connection, the unexpected chance for romance, aware that she was examining more middle-aged men in these minutes than she normally would in a month. She flashed a sidelong look at a black-haired, fine-boned UPS driver who definitely made her wish she had a package to sign for. How ridiculous. Cars and trucks slid past, each person enclosed within their car's bubble-effect. They weren't on drives in search of love; they drove like they were at war. So many people, here and there, alone, high-strung, strung out.

In her one-bedroom apartment, she shed her blue suit, ripped off her hose, and slipped into her wonderful old puffy bathrobe. Her legs ached from a day in pumps. She poured some red wine, and stretched out on her bed, ready to relax before the boob tube. She fingered the stem of her glass, looking for an empty spot to rest it on her night stand. She took a closer look at the remote control, lying there. The sound and channel buttons were arranged in a double line along the top of the 'gun'. Its sides had a heavy, rounded, actual hand gun quality. She lifted it; it was light, no hefty feel of consequence. Bang! she shot the plump bathrobed woman reflected in the green rounded TV screen. The woman stared firmly back, eyebrows raised, waiting for a good channel to click her out of the picture. Ah, Kate noted, even the appliance industry thought it fun to play cops and robbers, and send you shooting into your show.   This was as good a proof as any for how society treated life and death like a game. She'd show her composition classes; from her own bedroom, look!

She slept blithely, pleased with her plan. In the morning she stuck the remote in her purse. Taking the elevator down to the parking garage, she felt weird and silly and wanted to crack a joke, but her fellow neighbors looked tired and indifferent. What was she giddy about anyway?

Driving to class this Friday, she reminded herself of her physical weakness, her new issue with orifices.   Every morning she took a double dose of Gas-Lax and, all day, she squeezed her buttocks like a vice. *Poor invisible women, we middle-aged ones, underpaid. Trying to control what we reveal.*

Kate walked into the class.   She had not yet removed her coat, and there sat an essay already on her desk; "The NRA: The Real Means To Control Violence." The student's eagerness was a good sign. Yet a quick review of his piece revealed that Americans must: "Get the enemy before the enemy gets us. The NRA is pre-emptive. People are weak.   Someone should have admitted that kid needed to be locked-up. Look what they got for waiting!"   Kate quickly commented in the margin that his argument was rhetorically incomplete without proof, he must refute other positions so as not to be thought one-dimensional. He would probably not understand; most students thought their writing accomplished if written in a wave of passion. True, it was rare enough to get them to do that, but her job was to show there were further critical steps.

Lifting her hands like an invoking priest, gluteus clasped to gluteus to avoid any afflatus, she urged them deeper into the argumentative essay by asking, "You're new young citizens; what about this country makes you angry?"   In the back, a couple of students lost the struggle to stay awake, eyelids shut, their necks jolting back. "Come on, class, what infuriating moments have remained embedded in you?" Two young women in the second row stared as if lobotomized at a fixed point on the blackboard. Kate urged: "Try to remember..."!

Mike, bless him, had finished his first essay with an excellent revision. He raised his hand. He said his new title was: "What You See Is Not What You Get: the Hidden Motives Behind Violence." He elaborated: "There's fear in admitting you lack something. Like not owning Abercrombie & Fitch stuff, like that's a moral failure, see? You react by striking at those – the haves– who accept this hunger-making system, the inequity in the capitalist marketplace.   Maybe that guy killed his classmates because they bought into their sense of superiority."

"Thus our abundance of many material goods hurts us?" Kate encouraged. "Makes us targets? Maybe we deserve such violence?"

A Greek girl whose posture, hair and clothes were always perfect, rebutted,

"Ah, why shouldn't we be comfortable? No way. It's the murderers' parents that are to blame."

Mike raised his hand. Did the word: fart, *fart*, **fart**, occasionally run through his mind in a trill? One gem like him appeared rarely enough in a class, like hope out of Pandora's box. Kate shied from his stare. A drop of sweat trickled from her armpit. Her dignity was frail.

She turned the conversation to plot line; "Ladies and gents, after you state your ideas clearly, to yourself, on paper, ask the essential human question; does this present predict anything about our future? We know students are killing each other; what does this mean for us beyond today? What should we do? Your essay should not be a soliloquy. It must engage -- with place, action, or argument. Basically, move me! Get me to dialogue."

Then she remembered, "Let me show you!" And she yanked the remote control out of her purse, pointing with the barrel. Students leapt out of their chairs. Someone yelled, "Duck! Duck!" The Greek girl froze, a marble statue, screaming one long paralyzed "OOOOOOOOO...". A guy moaned on the ground at her feet.

Kate shouted, "It's a remote! A remote!" quickly realizing that meant nothing to them. "It's not real!" They stared back, mouths wide, dumbfounded. "I'm so sorry," she said. "That was very stupid. I wanted to make a point about – well, how in America even a TV control looks like a gun. It's part of a proliferating disease, see? Everyone come up here, touch it. See?" No one moved. "I got this as a promotional gift." She dangled it from her fingertips, as her breath rasped out in heaves. "The appliance industry likes to make death into a game. See?" Not even Mike spoke to her. She had planned to show them the remote, but not quite this way.

"Okay, okay, that's enough for today. Everyone dismissed." They shuffled out of class, glaring at her, though she was letting them out ten minutes early. Maybe all they saw was that she was crazy.

She walked out of the building alone; there was often no one around at this time. But Friday traffic was dependably bad. This month's first humid heat sidled up under her clothes. It pulsed through her half-open windows. She couldn't afford a car with air conditioning. Trucks cranked and churned at her ear level. Her hair gummed to her cheeks. Her lower back matted into to the upholstery. She fished in her purse for a mint, to distract her mouth if nothing else. Struggling to get through her jammed purse, she jerked out the awful remote, plopping it on the passenger seat, away from her. What a fiasco. How she would love right now to calm herself. Put on an instrumental CD, sit cross-legged, Zen-like, in a cool air-conditioned interior. The awfulness of her bad day and this crowded road no longer touching her. Hah! Kate started singing:

Headed on the highway,
Looking for adventure,
And whatever comes our way
Thank God I'm gonna make it happen...

She pounded out *Steppenwolf* on the steering wheel.

Nearing Chicago, the traffic crawled to ten miles an hour. Still an asshole started tailing her, pressing his big SUV inches from her Honda. Flashing his brights. If *she* suddenly braked, which she wanted to do, he'd splinter her hatchback, but his SUV would stay clean as a whistle. Not a feasible plan. Finally, finally, he veered into the next lane, achieving the great success of coming parallel to her. One of the test questions she gave her students was: *A parallel construction is:_____*. Context changed that answer, didn't it?

The *Steppenwolf* lyrics she'd been singing brought back that movie. Those confederates in their nasty pick-up lifted their shot guns and *Blam*! End of the *Easy Rider*. Had the asshole next to her ever seen that movie? She looked over at his fleshy face; she couldn't make out his age. A man with a big gas guzzler and a big attitude, Mr. Important. She lifted her remote, and pointed it at him.

He wasn't the type to look around and explore the environment, but the traffic was killer slow. It took about three minutes before he glanced her way, and saw the gun pointed at his head.

He slowly lifted his hands off the steering wheel. He turned them to her, in surrender, palms stationed flat open beside each ear. His lips pulled taut like elastic bands. Sunglasses hid his eyes. He began a head-shaking "no" motion. Then, sprung like a rocket, he was flying out the passenger side. From her rearview mirror, she could see him, round, in a flapping tan jacket, running in the line between cars like a marathoner. Traffic gradually surged ahead, but his driverless SUV remained. Angry honking blasted up his lane. Kate accelerated away. From her rearview, she watched cars swerve tensely out of the jammed lane. Just how far would Mr. SUV run?

Suddenly she felt beneficent. She'd stopped a jerk from pushing her around. When she reached her parking garage, she energetically greeted two elderly neighbors, and chatted amiably with the balding janitor with whom she rode the elevator. At home, she let Vanna White parade around the channel she'd mistakenly clicked on. Kate remembered reading about a bank robbery in which it was later discovered that the thief's gun was made out of plywood, just cloaked by a rag. What was possible in this world, as of yet! Hah!

In June, Kate began teaching her summer course, a class directed toward students whose provisional acceptance to college depended on catching up to the required fundamentals. Their writing would be re-tested at the end of summer. She didn't try out essays on violence with them.

There'd been a bit of a to do regarding the incident in her spring class, but her years of devotion and her clear explanation of the intent behind displaying her remote had reassured the administration that the students had misunderstood her. Nothing else in her record disproved them. It was over.

Students' failures in writing could usually be traced straight back to their high school teachers who, having discerned the time it took to grade papers, avoided assigning any. Occasionally, these kids discovered that the discipline in language that Kate demanded helped them to find themselves. They carved sentences to make their new voices. But others continued to toss smudged papers onto her desk, as careless as any teacher who might have brought them to this. These were minds like brick walls. She tossed possibilities at them. They bounced right to the floor. What gave her her faith in writing?

In July, she would enjoy her vacation. For two years now, Kate had reserved the same retreat; a little cottage up in Michigan, with a view of a pretty blue lake right through the stands of oak trees. She relished the patterns she assumed there. Sleep late, meander to the White Raft café for a heated blueberry scone and frothy coffee. Go back to the cottage. Pack up some books and slip on her black bathing suit. Head to the little beach. Kate never minded the noise of families around her because she happily insulated herself with her summer books under the hot sun. She did everything slowly; walked slowly, bathed slowly, ate slowly— and at the end of a couple of weeks she felt like a pleasant person through and through. Here, she had discovered the secret to rejuvenation.

She taught these summer courses because they were a worthy cause *and* she got paid a premium. That very premium enabled her escape. Tit for tat. Pleasure's price.

She had two more sweltering weeks to go. This afternoon, she approached her Honda, languidly removing her summer jacket. She dreaded her entry into the car's furnace. Plus, she had forgotten! Her TV waited, stuffed into her back seat; she was bringing it to Sears for repairs. The reception had taken to swerving large undulating waves, nothing else, like it was wired on psychedelic drugs. She headed into the general traffic. It flowed pretty quickly this afternoon. She wiped her forehead, and hummed. What was tonight's TV special? The biography of Jackie O.? All at once, she jammed her brakes. Some moron zipped his white van in a forceful diagonal, millimeters from her headlights. He got ONE space in front of her. For Christ's sake, they were almost at the toll booth. As she neared the tolls, she saw that to her left the toll line was shorter. She turned into it with a slight sense of triumph. Unfortunately, Mr. Van Asshole's profile was stopped to her right. This commute was clearly taking its toll on her; why care about these creeps? She concentrated on breathing deeply, trying to inhale spiritual healing and restraint. A couple of minutes later, she unfortunately glanced over and this same pervert opened his fleshy mouth to flick his tongue at her like a pulsing snake. A regular Mr. X-rated.

As if hard-wired to her memory, her purse seemed to speak: *Remember?* She clenched her fist. Mr. X winked. She gave him the finger. He responded by fucking *his* finger in and out of a hole made by his thumb and forefinger. Still stuck in her lane, with the culprit mouthing away next to her, why was she resisting? Out came the remote she was delivering with the TV to Sears. As they moved up, one car away from their respective turns to pay at the toll booths, he expressly mouthed: *you cunt.* He met the sight of her supposed gun pointed at his fat head. His hands flung up: this must be a normal first response. His dark eyes doubled in size. He lifted his palms up and down more times, as if he were praying to Allah. Then the car he was behind paid and the gate lever rose. All at once, Mr. Van Asshole accelerated, as if he could zoom out the same block. He screeched forward, but the descending toll arm was faster. It crashed on the roof of his van. The red-and-white striped arm half dragged the van, scraping it into the adjoining toll lane. A siren pierced the air. A police car parked on the highway shoulder immediately approached at a speedy perpendicular across all lanes, lights — blue, red, white — flashing, skidding to a stop.

Everything went into absolute stasis, every car and toll booth paralyzed. The cop jammed his arm into the van and yanked out Middle-Aged Fat-Pants, pressing the Asshole's arms against the van, beginning a weapons search. Kate sweated, and not only from the heat. She shoved her remote deep into her briefcase stuffed with student papers. All those pages that questioned her meaningfulness. Her breathing became labored. Another police car zoomed over; two cops leapt out. Kate kept her head low. After about ten minutes, the cops looked around. They waved the booths back open.

Kate paid her fare. Her hands shook, but she clucked, "Unbelievable!"

The attendant, labeled Wanda, leaned over, "How can they think they'll get away with it? What planet are they on?"

"Hard to tell," Kate nodded and drove off.

She moved into the right lane. Her arms shook; she did not think she could drive, but she must. The beneficence and sense of completion she had felt when she had done this once before did not reappear. She saw the huge sky, her smallness under it. The flat Midwest. It ended in haze at the horizon, like a view through a strip of scotch-tape. No hopeful distant hills. The tapering sky expanded upon itself until it got tired. It was tired now, indigo at its top center, then rosy, like warm skin, but frayed and sticking at its far edges. A V of Canada geese flew over, honking. When she was a kid in school, they had learned the geese were heroic long-distance travelers. These days, the geese were shortening that journey. They skipped the long haul to Canada and stayed around Chicago, got fat and comfortable, took over people's yards, peeing and defecating. They ruined lawns and ate cemeteries' commemorative flowers. So even Nature liked short cuts. Those geese must have felt a flurry of brilliance when they realized they could abort all that strain. At this very moment, she realized she must take the next exit. That jerk might describe her car to the police. How stupid, how stupid she was.

Her realization occurred that much too late. In her rearview, she could see a police car growing closer, flashing its blue lights.

She would not have any of this. She did not know beforehand she wouldn't, but she suddenly was sure. Whatever their interrogation, they would not understand. She floored the accelerator.

Who would have thought a Honda had so much pick-up? Its insect-size proved an asset. She swerved, ducking around cars easily, as of yet so unafraid it surprised her. But this *was* the other half of her dreams; to live as intensely as in a movie, in a car chase scene, the wicked heroine, her warm flesh powerfully invincible. Which reminded her; not one person, in that mess of traffic, with the police car chasing her, was thinking to himself: is she likely to fart? Nope, that was sure. That, she had gotten past.

When the Universe Anoints You Master of the Obvious

by Kevin Stein

You're the sudden deity of docile fact, immune to irony.

    Here's you at school solving the prose-poem conundrum,

"Poetry is verse, fiction is prose," students scribbling notes

    within the hallowed Norton. No one asks,

"Will this be on the test?" They've earned the Bachelors of Obviosity –

    you owning both the Masters and Ph.D. plus post-doc.

How comforting the known in any quadratic equation!

    Here's you in the grocery's Fast Lane

carting exactly ten items and your Kroger Bonus Card,

    you tipping the bag boy who drives a black BMW.

Here's you behind the wheel of the TV-movie "Beautiful Sunset,"

    script composed by twenty monkeys in a Yahoo! chat room,

meaning you're on the tollway with proper change,

    a full tank, and the notion Oprah's not going to marry

Stedman as you won't wed the actress with collagen lips.

    Here's you with hands at ten and two,

so D means Drive, Air says windows up but cool,

and today, my friend, the speedometer's 69 winks

"Easy, tiger, you'll get a ticket." Evening shoulders

the windshield as a bird's tweedle-dee

defines a tree. No need to solve for N.

Title

by Richard Jones

The Lost Son,
published in 1948,
is full of poems
I love—
"Moss-Gathering,"
"Big Wind,"
"My Papa's Waltz,"
"Flower Dump."
In 1953, the year
I was born,
The Waking
contained the beautiful
"Elegy for Jane,"
a poem I needed again
this morning to heal.
Roethke's titles alone—
Words for the Wind,
Praise to the End—
inscribe the mind,
inscribe the heart
with echoing cries
of stone, leaves, roots, wind.

Waiting for My Father to Die

by Richard Jones

I'm watching television with my daughter, who loves children's shows on PBS that spell out words— *behind...   beyond... become...* — words that to her father are heralds divining the future, or dispatch riders with reports from the forgotten past. The letters on the screen are lifted up by owls or tigers. It is all like a dream, the way the word *being* blows apart, the letters drifting away like falling leaves. *Believe. Belong.* I half expect the giraffe to say *beau ideal*, to teach my three-year-old the principles of excellence, the paradigms of beauty. On the television screen I see the ghost of my reflection, a face old and haggard, but then I see it is the day after tomorrow, and we are sitting by my father's grave, my daughter and I joined by the animals and the letters. And because she loves to read to her father, my daughter climbs into my lap and opens the black book—

And I heard
and I saw
and *behold—*
a white horse.

Teacher Is Gone
C.S.Felver, 1917-2006

by Paul Zimmer

Damn the years.
Damn the sudden dark.
Damn the light
That has gone away.

Words, shapes, colors,
Sounds—he taught
Them all to me
And made me glad,
But did not take time
To warn me of the void.

Teacher is gone at last.
And here I am myself—
Seventy-two years old.
What can I do now?
How do I do the rest?

Singing

by Joseph Hurka

For Andre Dubus

Today at Bradford College the sun was bright outside the windows of Hemingway library, the beautiful green of the trees a ripple of spring leaves. Lake Tupelo was sedentary, with layer upon layer of silt on the shore, water settling down for a dry summer, leaving a trail of itself like layers of salt left behind an ancient sea.

There is, for me, always in these leaves at Bradford College, always in this sunlight on water, always you, Andre. You were there today, and in the winter before your death you were there, on frozen evenings as students studied in the warmth of the library. One winter night I saw them through the windows as I walked to Hemingway; they sat at their desks in brightly-colored sweaters, protected from the winter blue outside. I stopped a moment, surrounded by pale snow and skeletal iced trees, remembering.

On that same winter walkway years before you'd asked me, how would I describe those trees? I gave you words and you gave me singing, a song, spirit – a way to make those trees come alive so that today I still see them, the winter night glow of them, the clicking of their branches when wind picked up. We stood before the trees and you taught me: you talked about Faulkner's great, quiet power and we spoke of our love for *The Wild Palms* and *As I Lay Dying*. We walked with Chekhov's Vassilyev one winter night in 1889, imagining in the face of a prostitute a martyr. You said: *obey Flaubert: use always the precise word. Take your time with your stories, live with your characters.* You said: *the secret is to know exactly what your character is thinking before your pen leaves the page.* As I stood there and watched your deep, sensitive face looking into the winter night, the dimensions of my life changed. I had lived in a small, contained room and you opened up a wall of that room and there was the universe: mystery and majesty.

And then, Andre, on a February night seventeen years later, you stepped into that universe.

I am sometimes frightened of this place you are in. I am a little ashamed of this, for you are with infinity, and I should not be afraid of any place that you are. But I find myself comforted by the first light of morning, by routine. I pour orange juice, I open the window blinds to light, to my neighbor's yard. I hear the sounds of people getting ready for work, conversations about what they'll do in the evening, water running and crockery being set back in cupboards. I close my eyes and see infinity as a great celestial curve: there are stars beyond. I feel fear and I open myself to it: I hear your joyful singing and laughter. You are there and whatever this is, your love is there. This is your final lesson to me, the final one of so many lessons that keep on teaching me – to not let this go, to not simply believe again in the ordinary, in a life of routine, mortal blindness.

In the afternoon today I drove from Bradford College back through the spring day with its late sun. At home I watched the bright, insistent block of television and listened to the news it gave me: of a northwestern tribe once again hunting whales, as their ancient ancestors had done; of children roaming through schools with guns and terror. You would have hated this news of school violence: sometimes I think you went before all of those children so that you could be there for them when they came, bewildered, to the stars. I switched off the television and read through passages of Jaroslav Seifert's *The Casting of Bells*, looking for this: *The dead live one more moment through those tears and are then more beautiful than when they lived.*

Women talk beneath my window now, as I write: they are happy to see one another. Their voices are a civil, intelligent song, a moment of grace. I think of how Seifert speaks of them, too, of their lives rocking to phases of the moon. *This is the ancient curve of life*, he writes, *of love and blood.*

You dance there now, in the place of love and blood, the world of women that you loved, Andre. You sing from the ancient curve. I hear you when I watch the trees and water, and the night with its crescent moon; I raise the voice you found in me, and take up my pen, and I sing with you.

Lesson

by Richard Jones

I sit on a rock
at the end of the lane
waiting for the bus to bring my boys
home. And while I sit
I inventory thoughts
and judge most of what is
in my head
to be meaningless noise.
I shake the pebbles of the mind;
the tin can of my skull rattles.
As I sit on the rock
and look harder, deeper,
I hum a tune
and realize it's Dylan—
every man's conscience
is vile and depraved.
Then it seems I am predestined
to think of John Calvin,
the doctrine of Total Depravity—
man did not merely fall,
but exists now in a black state
of absolute corruption and wickedness.
The afternoon sun
suddenly hotter,
I'm tempted
to ask for freedom
from the thoughts a man thinks,
when the leviathan
of the yellow school bus
rounds the corner
and spews my children from its belly.
Walking the narrow lane home,
I listen to lessons
the boys learned at school.
William recites in a song

the names of the continents,
Andrew counts
from one to ten in Japanese,
and together they insist
even I
might learn
with a small scapel
and a pair of tweezers
how to dissect a frog
to further study its tiny heart.

Working Out with Austin

by Philip Dacey

Once fathers and sons worked
the land together.
Now they spot
for each other working
with free weights.

They share a new language--
pectoral fly, low/rear delt,
lat pulldown--as they lift
the weight of the past
and transfer it

to the future.
The Y is where they meet.
Why. Because. Because of heat--
paternal, filial.
Just watch them sweat.

Stretched out
on the abs bench after me,
Austin strengthens himself
in the ghost of my warmth.
Abs for absence?

Then he teaches me the lunge:
on one knee, as he thinks
quads, I think
my boyhood genuflections,
submissions.

The Hot Stinking Truth of the Matter, or
Welding Basics for Poets

by Steven Sherrill

Listen, I grew up breaking things open to see how they worked. You'll have to believe me when I say that I was much better, more focused, and more intuitive at tearing things apart than I was at putting them back together. Still am. Back then, when I thought spending my PELL Grant on a rock climbing harness and a blue rope was the right decision; back when I regularly cut North Carolina to the bone on a variety of motorcycles, I had little doubts about my manhood. Now two decades later, having evolved (that's the hopeful spin) into a namby-pamby poet-slash-novelist-slash-English Professor, I sometimes forget that hard-edged boy.

But things change. Always. And time often shuns the yardstick for the much sexier Möbius strip. You'll be going along, living your current life, feeding your fat dog, marking on student papers, squeezing in an occasional indie flick, and some unexpected little detail will creep up, grab your skinny ass, and hurl you backwards in time.

A clean weld does just that for me.

My first academic success was in a community college welding program. Partly out of defiance, and partly out of default, I had eschewed the natural familial progression in my Southern lineage, that of a life in the textile mills— a swing-shift life of lint heads, brown lung, and the maddening clack clack clack of the looms. Sheer boredom, and too much Gilligan's Island, drove me to Mitchell Community College where their propaganda promised rewards and riches beyond my imagination, or, at the very least, a skill and a career.

I perused the options. At the lofty Associate Degree level Accounting, Business Administration, Criminal Justice, Early Childhood, and Medical Assisting counterbalanced the —lowest— Certificate choices of Accounting (Yes, Accounting.), Air Conditioning/Heating & Refrigeration, Basic Law Enforcement, Cosmetology, TV-VCR Repair, Nursing Assistant. But it was along the middle path, among the gussied-up Diploma programs, that I first experienced the hankering for the arc struck and sustained. Accounting (Yes, Accounting!), Air Conditioning/Heating & Refrigeration, Cosmetology, Electrical/Electronic, Medical Assistant, and Welding.

Welding. Whoa! Slow down big boy! Welding.

While there's no arguing that it's dirty hot smelly work, lord have mercy, nothing said Manly like welding. I was seduced by the trappings: the bulbous gray mask, capable of blocking all but the most insistent light; the thick leather gauntlets; and, best of all, the power. The welder, with his hands full of fire, had the power to join the most resistant surfaces on earth. Had the power to pierce the seemingly impenetrable, to reduce hard hard metals to momentary liquid and bring them back together in a new (better, more functional, aesthetically improved) form.

Sign up I did. I threw myself heart and soul into my studies. Bolstered by the courage imparted to me through the slag hammer and wire bristle brush, I faced my fears. I learned. I learned so much. I learned about electrical current. I understood (more or less) the properties of metal, and I'm talking at the atomic level. I could identify all the various joints: butt, corner, lap, T, and edge. I knew what made a good bead, the weld itself, even if I couldn't always lay one. I bandied about terms like *electrode* and *flux, oxy-acetylene* and *inert gas* as if I owned them.

I went to the cafeteria for lunch every day with welding rods jammed into my back pocket, because I thought the girls would think it cool. I studied, a practice not in my nature, but even more than studying, I looked ahead. All that cart-before-the-horse business. I fancied myself not just a welder but a *specialist*. Let's make a sports analogy. If, for instance, everyday welders, the guys who do repairs and build things in the fabrication shops out by the interstate, if those men are bowlers, then pipe-welders are the quarterbacks and big league pitchers of the industry. I don't even know enough about sports to make a comparison with underwater welders, but that's where I had my sights set.

The Mitchell Community College welding program was rigorous and demanding. Sort of. Each student had to choose a final project, and have that project approved by our instructor. With supportive skepticism, my plans to build an aluminum johnboat (start to finish; the whole damn thing) were okayed. Why an aluminum johnboat? I cannot begin to answer that question. I didn't fish. I didn't even swim. Water made me nervous. Still does.

At the end of that final quarter, I borrowed my uncle's pickup truck and hauled the boat, along with my impressive GPA, home where it sat— with its beads progressing from sloppy and irregular where I started building, to pretty damn smooth by the last few seams— on sawhorses in the back yard until I sold it to a friend I used to get high with. Somewhere, though, I have a Polaroid of the boat, floating in a lake of weeds and brambles behind my parents' house.

Before you get too excited, I need to tell you that I never worked as a welder. Not for one single minute.

Mercifully, for both me and the industrial world, when I graduated there was a recession in full swing. Just how I got from there, tradesman sans job/mit diploma, to here, Professor Steve, muckraker of words, is too convoluted a story to tell in this article. Suffice it to say that my superhero name is Impressionable Boy.

I'll tell you, though, that while I have forgotten most of what I learned in welding school, I can no longer read blueprints; amps and volts confuse me; some things I will never forget. Some things linger and even grow. I am sure we didn't have a lesson on *faith* anywhere in my four quarters of study. But faith is what I've come away with. I know, now, that sometimes, in order to understand a thing (a piece of metal pipe, a desire, a fear, a love), you have to go so far inside it, you have to commit yourself so fully and intensely to the thing that it melts, puddles, opens like a round mouth of fire, and you can't know how things will resolve on the other side of that fiery moment until you try.

There is a recurring moment in the welder's life, a brief dark instance just before each new weld, when the big gray mask, the über-head, is flipped into place and all goes black. There is no sense of light, and only the sound of one's own breath, until the arc is struck. It is faith in the arc that sustains us. I still carry things in my pockets to impress the girls. It's mostly a metaphor by now, but no less ridiculous. I don't like to get my hands dirty anymore. But a pretty weld can pull me right out of my soft reality. I finger beads of all kinds. Expensive bicycle frames. Stair railings. Poles. Stainless steel tables in those fancy Manhattan restaurants. When I come across a particularly nice weld, I'll trace my finger along its full length, and there's more give and take than I can explain in the experience. I've come to understand that just as there is a time for seamlessness, it's often necessary for the seams to show.

This past year, on the campus where I teach, where I grow soft and tenure-able, a new building is under construction. Every day I'd come to work to find more and more steel girders rising up out of the Pennsylvania muck and jutting skyward. And, as if that wasn't goad enough, it seemed that my passing the job site— on the way to the copy center or the coffee shop— always coincided with some tough welder's diesel engine throttling up. Mercy, mercy, the sounds of the laboring, straining engine, the fiery arc sputtering hissing and spitting like a microcosmic sun storm, the sounds of a welding machine hard at work went deep, took hold of those fabricators of noise tucked in my inner ear— the hammer, anvil, and stirrup— and refused to let go.

I've watched these men, hard at work, for nearly a year now. Watched the building come up out of the earth and take solid rectangular shape. I've enjoyed it, really I have. But there's no denying the struggle. There is no sense in pretending that every time the arc is struck in my presence it is all I can do, all I can do, all I can do, not to jump into my clean Passatt, rush the half mile home, turn my closets upside down until I find that faded and wrinkled Polaroid of my aluminum boat, the one I welded, take that picture back, shinny up a steel pole and yank on that man's leather sleeve until he turns, raises his mask, and hears me say it. The picture thrust in his face, I'll say it until he believes me.

"See! Do you see this! I made it! I made it."

Mr. A

by Frederik Pohl

For the author of some of the most touching verse in the English language, and some of the meanest-minded.

When Mr. A was a schoolboy
    He fagged for the upper form.
He learned to like their customs,
    And fagging became his norm.

People called him "pervert."
    People called him "gay."
They thought he loathed all womankind,
    And that was true of Mr. A.

He viewed old maids with revulsion—
    Scent, taffeta, and dust.
He thought their sorrows comic.
    For their persons, just disgust.

Yet deep inside his sharp-tongued self
    In the place where he made his art,
He owned a wise and tender eye
    And a soft and fragile heart.

Mr. A set the parts of grammar
    Into artful, sweet designs,
And taught us to share the loves he bore
    In a thousand lovely lines.

How prankish God must be, to stretch
    And open from above
The heart of this mean-mouthed cynic
    So utterly to love.

The Plugs

by William Heyen

On August 6, 1945, shortly after the *Enola Gay* rose from its runway on Tinian Island in the Pacific, Morris Jepson descended into the bomb bay to commence arming our weapon nicknamed "Little Boy."

This is what I read this morning in a newspaper. Jepson changed the bomb's "plugs," then the *Enola Gay* rose to 30,000 feet & at 8:15 a.m. its pilot, Col. Paul W. Tibbetts, gave the order, & that was that, 90,000 dead soon after, another 145,000 within months, etcetera.

I'm thinking about this 60 years later. If you're like me, you're too numb from all our wars to care, or care very much, but those plugs, metal or hard rubber, whatever shape they were & however many, whether threaded into apertures or hammered into place or welded, whatever size they were, do interest us—their occluded density, the gagged occluded sound of them, their color, how they might have felt in Jepson's hands, their metallic or rubbery odor in his mind as he concentrated on his task, as the American weapon assumed its consequential form. Before now, no poem or prose piece has received them, has welcomed these plugs in their material innocence, their muteness, in their full utilitarian nature, home. They served us, parts of the whole, & having served us, when "Little Boy" detonated 1,890 feet above the city, our plugs disappeared into the micro-afterdust of uranium, into almost nothingness.

Almost. Except that we breathe these microcosmic particles, our lungs filter & distribute these plugs minute by minute, breath by breath.

The *Enola Gay* sailed through the atomic flash & got back to its base. The plane still exists, entire, itself another dimension of plug, the names of its 12-man crew stenciled on its fuselage. I haven't yet seen it, but maybe will, on exhibition in the Smithsonian or wherever it will be. But whether or not I ever see it, or you ever see it, doesn't much matter. What matters is that word with which Jepson was working & which we cannot/will not forget or replace.

The next time you push a plug into a socket. The next time you fish for bass or pickeral with a plug. The next time you hear a plug for a politician. Hold the word in hand &/or mind. Hiroshima. *Guh*, at the back of the throat. *Guh*. August 6, 1945. Morris Jepson changes "Little Boy's" plugs.

The Rape of Nanking

by David Mura

There's a ladybug on the window
and I keep raising, lowering
to sweep it away. The hills
of the South Bay, eucalyptus
and pine. Deer and bobcats, million
dollar mansions, and all
I can recall are my interviews,
prisoners jailed by the Japanese,
whippings, cigarette
butts to genitals, slices
of skin peeled off as if
unveiling an orange (and this
just those who survived).
I add these memories
to corpses stacked like a club
sandwich of death, days, weeks of it,
in the streets of Nanking. The earth
a raw maw for the spineless
Chinese who cried out, begging
in ways no soldier
of Nippon could conceive,
though they could conceive
how to rape any female
they came across, how to mate
two neighbors or a sister and a brother
in public, before the village,
on their march towards massacre
and the meat of China.
                              I turn
off 17, past the Cat restaurant,
up a private road, the ladybug
still at the window till
at last my fingers seize it,
cracking the shell, liquid oozing out
like some strange sampler candy

and I foist the stain to my nostrils,
the waft electric, a wire over-
heated and smoking.
                            I'm there,
now, no traffic, thickets up
the hillside, and a hum in my brain
draws up the face of the old G.I.
who, spying my face at the door
for an interview, curses out "Jap"
as I back away and flee....
                            Fumbling
I pull it from my purse. Ah,
now I understand it. That phrase—
dead weight. The dead weight
of all those pages I wrote or
the phone ringing in the dead
of night, slightly Asian, slightly
British—"If you persist...."
I want this story, I want this story,
I told myself, knowing
no apology would ever suffice.
Silly girl, you're even a Nip to some,
a Chink to others. History's over,
isn't that what Fukuyama said?
I place the barrel to my temple
and see the sky of Nanking,
faceless soldiers standing above me,
shoving us into earth,
and I am there, tumbling
towards darkness. I smell them
on my hands, crush them with
my weight. Cry out once
like the banshee they say I am
and quickly squeeze the trigger.

Four Variations on A Theme

by S.L. Wisenberg

1.
In New Haven
and Palo Alto
Milgram and Zimbardo
took the measure of Homo sapiens,
calibrating obedience
and cruelty
in their labs. They watched
as "normal" subjects
set in motion
punishment and simulated death.
Zimbardo shut down a pretend
prison in a Stanford basement
a week early
when one-third of his volunteer guards
went too far. Pacifists turned
sadists and the good professor
found himself transformed. <u>The evil
situation triumphs
over good people.</u>

* * *

Take the hand
of the mass murderer
and follow the rivers
etched in his palm. They'll lead you
to a source you cannot name
as something
apart.

2.
The rich buy their excuses
in the open market,
pour all the perfume
of Araby
over their guilt,
hoping that no one can recognize
their scent.

3.
The historian Browning, seeking
the reverse alchemy
that changed
reservists from Hamburg
into mass killers in Poland,
emerged from the Nazi archives
with "great unease." He titled his book
"Ordinary Men" and looked to
Milgram and Zimbardo
for maps of the human
heart. As he sifted
through files, grown brittle
with time, the screams of My Lai
echoed.

4.
When was the day
you stopped
wringing your hands
and then
what did you
do?

Notes: "Evil" quote is a paraphrase of Zimbardo.

Keats at Bedtime

by Philip Dacey

I'm showing off the recent
acquisition of "Ode to Autumn"
by my brain and heart, reciting
face to face, our heads on pillows,
my voice gone Brit-plummy.

Now in our harvest years,
we've just harvested
each other, her recent sounds
"treble soft," mine more
"loud bleat," and she's sleepy

but encouraging of this
second performance or encore.
My roving hand underscores
"bosom-friend" and "ripeness,"
"touch" and "hair soft-lifted."

We know we are "the next swath"
the hook spares, and our "twined
flowers" are children and friends,
certain places, the daily round.
With our own "gathering swallows"

circling near, casting shadows
like thoughts weighted
toward winter, we burrow
deeper, the words like snow falling
on eyelashes as her eyes close.

Jasmine Dream

by Kenneth Pobo

As I drink reheated coffee,
and answer e-mail, you

sleep. Out the window,
a winter jasmine, oh so
yellow, mellow but feisty,
sedate but kick-ass. No news
that I can send matches

this bush's just-breaking story.
Maybe you're dreaming in yellow,
blossoms surrounding your
sleep--your eyes open
and a day begins,

a yellow day, a hundred suns
no higher than my waist.

Glass Roots

by Kenneth Pobo

In western Pennsylvania, Stan and I
look at glass. Ruby. Cobalt blue. Depression era.
These words make us sing. Literally.
As we ponder and shop, he hums a doowop. I sing

"Do Something To Me" by Tommy James and the Shondells. Oh,
October 1968, a bicycle and licorice. I'm 14.
I hate school--"Pobo, he's a shoe," popular kids say.
I'm still a shoe. A glass vase. A record

spinning. A Reese's peanutbuttercup. Ammonia.
Half man, half trowel.
I grew up on Jesus and a lawn mower,
family and Melmac cups. My Villa Park, Illinois,

grade school became a retirement home. At 51,
I walk past it whenever I visit my parents.
The plane returns me to Philly.
Stan picks me up. We're plotting to overthrow

the American family. Everyone on the news says we are.
So it must be true.
We do radical things--
vacuum (OK, not too often),

work (he at Amtrak, me teaching),
and have Bette Davis-Gary Merrill battles
over hollyhocks and lilies (I'm being dramatic,
we can get huffy, but so far no storming out)--

I've needed almost half a century to put down
more lasting roots, to find a place by the window
where morning sun hits a glass vase just right
and makes it sparkle--even briefly--

before clouds come. Before a cat's tail
whaps it onto the floor. Unbroken, the vase waits
for the next morning's sun, a hummingbird
on a thin gold string, just above African violets.

The Replacement Padre

by Philip Gerard

L ate on Christmas Eve the young priest arrived at the St. Dismas Chapter House in a howling snowstorm clutching a single brown leather valise next to his body, as if it gave off warmth. In all his travels for the Vatican, he had never been to Chicago before and the wind tore through his flimsy trench coat and shivered his insides. He had walked almost twenty blocks from the train, not knowing any better, and his feet were numb inside Italian loafers and thin socks. He could feel the cold, iron shapes of his own bones as he stumped up the long stone staircase, leaving deep footprints, and pressed the lighted doorbell with the heel of his gloved hand.

Through the steamy sidelight a woman's red face glared at him and he quickly turned open the broad lapels of his black trench coat to reveal a Roman collar and the door at once opened with a sucking sound. Behind her in the warmth of a parlor somewhere he heard men's voices and smelled cherry pipe tobacco. The woman stood arms akimbo, a wiry redhead with mistrustful eyes. She was near his own age, thirty-two, though she held herself like an older woman who has been used to running a large household, at once motherly and aloof, with an aura of accumulated exhaustion around her narrow eyes and in the blue veins on the backs of her shiny red hands. She introduced herself as Mrs. Riordan. "You wouldn't be Father Tellum?"

"Kellum, yes," he said while she locked the door behind him. "Stephen Kellum."

"Then you'll be wanting a hot toddy, Father," Mrs. Riordan said as he shed his coat into her arms. "We expected you for supper. We had given up on you in this storm."

"Actually, just a cup of tea would be heaven."

"On Christmas Eve, Father?" And then seeing how he averted his eyes she understood. "Tea it is, then."

She showed him where to freshen up and then guided him to a cozy parlor where a large fire crackled in a deep hearth. Two priests and a seminarian sat in leather club chairs arranged in a semi-circle before the fire, sipping drinks and smoking, and the talk stopped abruptly as he filled the doorway with his tall frame.

"Another Christmas transient!" the chubby priest nearest him said. "Come, warm yourself at the fire." He shoved back his chair to make room, paddling it backward with his short legs without getting up, holding fast to a pipe. The seminarian stubbed out his cigarette in a brass ashtray, stood and made a fuss of offering his own chair to Father Kellum and then pulling up another, enlarging the semi-circle. The other priest, a very old man with a bent neck and hooded eyes, made no move but jiggled the ice in his glass, a signal for the chubby priest to fill it with more whiskey from a cut-glass decanter on a side table.

Father Kellum leaned into the fire and warmed the palms of his hands. They were so numb that at first the new circulation stung and then gradually the fire was in his blood and the sensation was thrilling. Outdoors, after so long in Italy, he had felt as if he had been walking for months and might never be warm again. Now he closed his eyes and absorbed the warmth, the tobacco smoke, and the aroma of hot tea. Mrs. Riordan draped his gloves over the steam radiator under the heavy-curtained window and he smelled the steaming wool and for just an instant craved a hot slug of whiskey to cap off his glow— but that impulse passed.

"I see you've met our Mary Rose," the chubby priest, whose name was Frammer, said. Mrs. Riordan smiled at being referred to in the familiar, set down a plate of fresh cakes and candies, and left the room.

"This is Vincent D'Onofrio, freshly ordained from St. Boniface." The seminarian offered his hand and Kellum expected a grip like a rugby player's but instead the handshake was cautious and brief. He looked limber and strong, with a Mediterranean face, and Kellum briefly wondered why he had taken the Orders, a handsome boy like that. The boy ducked his head shyly, and Kellum figured he knew.

The old priest was introduced as Malpass, and he did not shake hands.

"Welcome to limbo."

The Chapter House was a way station for priests in transit from one assignment to another, or in between postings. Occasionally priests were sent here because they had somehow gotten themselves into trouble and needed to be removed from parish work for awhile. They boarded at the Chapter House until it was determined what was to be done with them.

Father Frammer relit his pipe and sucked on it till it was going good and briefed Father Kellum. The seminarian was on his way to a parish outside St. Louis. Father Frammer himself had been here almost two years. He offered no explanation why. Father Malpass had arrived only day before yesterday, summoned by the bishop for an interview, but the interview had been postponed indefinitely and he had been told to remain at the Chapter House to await a young priest from the Holy See.

"And where would you be headed, Father?"

"Please— call me Stephen." He sipped his tea and considered. "Business."

Frammer waited but all at once seemed to understand he was going to get no more information than that.

"Well, at any rate, you're just in time for our Christmas Eve custom."

"And what custom would that be, Father?"

The old priest lifted his head, as if annoyed, and stared hard at Fr. Kellum. Fr. Frammer said, "Stories, Father. Each of us must tell a story that captures the spirit of Christmas. I'll go first."

Father Frammer lifted a glass and told a story about a young farmer in Maine, lost in the woods when his old car slid off the road while coming home on Christmas Eve with a trunkload of presents for his kids. He wandered in a full blizzard until he was nearly spent, then stumbled into the snow and lay face down. "Then, slowly, he got to his knees," Father Frammer said, his eyes alight with faith. "He prayed to the Virgin for deliverance-- not for himself, but for his family, who depended on him. A young wife, two small kids in that hard country. And when he had finished praying, he opened his eyes and lifted his head and lo and behold! A light!"

"And he followed that light, didn't he," said the seminarian, and Fr. Kellum couldn't tell if he meant irony or was just caught up in the foolish story.

"Indeed he did," Fr. Frammer went on. "And strange to say, there was nothing there at all. No fire or lantern. And yet he followed that light to his own doorstep."

"And there was no light at all?" said the seminarian.

"Just hope and the unexplained," Fr. Frammer said. They all drank and Fr. Kellum thought, My faith is not based on fairy tales in the woods.

"Your turn," Fr. Frammer said to Vincent D'Onofrio, the seminarian. D'Onofrio slicked back his dark hair with his hand and grinned a little self-consciously. He looked from one to the other with his expressive brown eyes as if seeking permission, and when they were all looking at him, he began his story. As he talked, his graceful olive hands made figures in the air. "A little boy in my home town during the time of polio, this is his story," he said. The tale took place in a hilltop church during midnight mass. "My older brother was serving the mass," Vincent D'Onofrio said. "The other altar boy was the brother of the kid who was crippled with polio."

The crippled kid wanted a sled for Christmas, he explained, that was how the story went. A sled for a crippled boy in a town where it had snowed only once in a decade. That Christmas Eve came the usual rain and the people of the afflicted town packed inside the little hilltop church impatient for the mass to be over, scared of their neighbors, sullen and without faith. The rows of wooden pews were stacked with crutches. Kids in leg braces sprawled across car coats and the whole service was a mockery of the Christmas spirit.

"And then at the end of the mass, Father Cruikshank– that was his name, an old-school pastor– flung open the rear doors of the church and the world was covered in fresh snow, a blizzard of snow." The memory seemed to make him happy and sad at once.

Fr. Malpass rattled his ice cubes and Fr. Frammer refilled his glass. Fr. Malpass reached inside the buttons of his cassock and fingered something on a chain around his neck. Fr. Kellum watched him.

"My father herded us all out the door fast, to get an early start down the hill." But the car slewed into a ditch. "My mother fell getting out of the car, broke her ankle clean," he said. "Then the crippled boy's father– I wish I could recall his name– he went to the trunk of his car and pulled out a sled, a present for the kid with polio. Can you believe it? The men used it to haul my mother back up the hill into the church and we all spent the night there, waiting for the snowplow.

"And when everybody had gotten settled down inside, this crippled kid and his brother and sister sneak out and they don't see me but I follow them out into the snow. And the brother and sister–" he was working his hands now–"they set this little crippled kid on the sled and they climb on in front and behind him and then off they all go down the hill.

"They must have done this half the night, and each time, the big brother, the altar boy, would haul the sled up the hill with his little brother on board, squealing with laughter. I watched them until my toes went numb and just before I went inside I noticed that Father Cruikshank had been standing there all along, in the shadow of the sacristy doorway, watching them, too. He looked my way his eyes were brimming with tears."

"That's a 'good one,' Fr. Frammer said, helping himself to a cake.

"It was like the pause," Vincent D'Onofrio said. "The pause just before the world starts up again." He looked away and shook his head and it was all so real to him, Fr. Kellum could see that. "That little kid, he didn't do so well. He never got to be a big kid. But that night. That night."

Vincent D'Onofrio was himself almost overcome with the memory. Fr. Kellum wondered if the story were even true. Why was the pastor crying? Was he moved by the naive faith of the children, by the older brother's obvious devotion to the crippled boy? Or was he crying because the boy was crippled, a pathetic little kid, like all the other dozens and hundreds in his town stricken with that mysterious affliction? Or because his parishioners had lost their faith? Or because he himself had lost heart? The story depressed him, inspired doubt rather than faith. Why did they all feel the tug of sentiment, the pull of a trumped-up happy ending in a world that offered none, not in this life? Why was pure faith not enough? It was only faith that consecrated action. He stared at the fire a moment.

Fr. Malpass turned abruptly from the fire and stared again at Fr. Kellum. "What do you want?" he said.

Fr. Kellum said nothing, sipped his tea.

"Why have you come? I know why you have come." His face colored with anger and his voice trembled. "What do you want?"

"Nothing."

"Nothing?"

The old priest deflated into his chair and loosened his Roman collar. He pulled the white plastic tab free of his cassock and laid it on the side table. "You're after this."

"Father!" said Fr. Frammer.

"I am eighty-two years old and I have no use for dissembling," Fr. Malpass said, his fingers once again inside the buttons of his cassock.

Fr. Frammer broke in, "Please, Father Malpass– it's your turn."

"Yes," Fr. Kellum agreed. "Tell us a story."

"So that's what you've come for," Fr. Malpass said. "All these years." He rattled his ice cubes and Fr. Frammer poured his glass so full that a little sloshed over the brim.

Fr. Malpass cast his eyes down, testing his words, as if he were not sure he should tell them, not here, not to these men. At last he nodded and said, "I am older than all of you and so this is an old-fashioned story."

"But a story of faith and deliverance, I'll bet," Fr. Frammer said.

"We'll just see about that." He sucked on his whiskey and didn't speak for a long moment, and nobody was sure he would continue, but at length he did. First he lifted his eyes and stared at the newcomer with a kind of disgust. "Once upon a time there was a replacement padre."

It was a time of madness, the old priest said. The War. Fifteen thousand men of a certain division had come ashore in June on the bloody beaches of Normandy and slogged their way inland across open fields hemmed in by berms nine feet high and brush so thick a man could not push through it, you had to blast your way through or push it down with a bulldozer tank.

"We lost men every day– cut down by hidden machineguns, pulverized by artillery fire. A third of those men were either dead or missing in action by the time we entered Paris in August. Five thousand." He paused and watched the new priest's eyes as if he were trying to scare him with a ghost story and wanted to know if it was working. He found nothing in his eyes. "'Missing'–that's a polite way of saying a man has been blown to bits and there is nothing left to recognize. Blood– and meat." He let it sink in. "And the soul is-- God knows where the soul is. They marched through Paris in a victory parade and the same day went back into the line, attacking west to the border of Germany."

It was a place called the Hurtgen Forest, he said. And by then the survivors were known as the "Bloody Bucket" division— on account of the red keystone shoulder patch they wore, the emblem of the Pennsylvania National Guard. And because they had shed so much blood.

By Thanksgiving they had lost another third of their men. "The reinforcements? Kids right out of high school. They died quick and easy, no trouble to anybody. Nobody even bothered to learn their names. What was the point?"

Fr. Frammer looked stricken. Vincent D'Onofrio gazed at the old priest in rapt wonder, as if he were some new species of life that he did not quite recognize. Fr. Kellum was picturing the scene: the haggard, exhausted infantrymen huddled in muddy holes covered by tree trunks against the airbursting artillery that shattered tree limbs into long jagged splinters that could cut a man in half. The relentless cold, the gray sky, the men hacking up phlegm and blood, their toes turning putrid and black and their feet yellow and mealy from trenchfoot. Shivering from a cold that would not stop. Coughing bloody pneumonia. No place to go indoors. No shelter. For weeks on end. Months.

"It was all dark forest. The enemy everywhere, anywhere, nowhere. Pass out in your hole, sunrise the guy in the next hole over has his throat cut and you didn't hear a thing. Didn't dare show themselves in daylight. Either side. Burrowed into the mud like rodents, killed when they had to. Knives, guns, bare hands. And died by the hundreds.

"And then the padre part?" Fr. Frammer's look went suddenly hopeful, as if he expected redemption to come along any minute. Fr. Kellum thought, well it's a bad business.

"The old padre, the unit chaplain, he was killed in the first days of fighting in the Hurtgen. What they called 'The Death Factory.' For it made one thing only. He would go foxhole to foxhole with the sacraments. A good man. A pious man. He would tend the wounded and comfort the dying. An airburst." He drank a slug whiskey. "He just evaporated. Just a bloody mist."

Fr. Kellum could see it and wished he too had whisky: The body liquefied, the soul gone in an instant.

"The new padre, what they called the replacement padre, he has this bright idea. It's coming up on Christmas Eve. Nobody knows that the Germans are breaking through all along the line."

Yes, Kellum thought. The Battle of the Bulge. They made movies out of it.

"These guys are on the dark side of the moon. Another planet. A cold planet, a planet without God."

Nobody spoke. For a priest to say that out loud.

"This replacement padre, he wants to say Christmas Eve mass. Now, this is a bad idea. As bad an idea as anybody ever heard of out there."

Father Frammer's face puckered as if he couldn't comprehend how mass could ever be a bad idea.

The old priest ignored him. "He comes up on the line, starts cajoling guys to come out of their foxholes, to crawl out from under their piles of tree trunks, and out into this little clearing. It's quiet as the grave. The Germans aren't doing anything. They're Catholics like us, he explains, with that goofy beatific look on his face.

"One by one, the guys start crawling out of the mud and standing up. The new kids first. The replacements. Kids. Because they believe. Want to believe. Something to hang onto. Some of them hadn't actually stood all the way up in days, weeks. They crawl and crouch and wriggle in the mud but they never stand upright, that's a death sentence."

"You were there," Fr. Kellum said quietly.

"And you weren't." Fr. Kellum knew what he was thinking: God damn you.

"Nevertheless." He paused for so long that Fr. Kellum doubted he would continue. But all at once the words came out of his mouth in a new voice, not so detached as before, a voice thick with emotion– what? Bitterness? Anger? Maybe grief.

"I had just come back on the line. Had a sort of, they called it an episode. Battle fatigue." He laughed without mirth. "They tell me– they said that when Andy–but you don't know Andy." He held his head, looked for a moment ancient and lost. "I woke up in the rear strapped to a cot."

Fr. Kellum knew how it was, for he had spent some time in research. His job in the Vatican. History. What was. How to learn from what was. Where the guilt lay. Where the redemption-- but there was rarely redemption. In that war, when a soldier came off the line with battle fatigue, they hustled him into a medical tent, pumped him full of sodium amytal– "blue eighty-eights," what they called the little pills, after a caliber of German cannon– and knocked him out for 24-48 hours, sometimes longer. Hot showers, the first they'd had in months, hot as they could stand, as long as they wanted. Clean sheets, no noise, all whispers, nothing but soft edges. The patients would thrash around in nightmares. Sometimes the staff would sit by the bed and goad them into remembering. "They're shooting at you. Look out! Here comes another barrage!"

This was thought to be good preventive medicine, make the patient deal with his fears. Get it out of his system now, like bleeding the air out of a brake line.

Then they'd hold him up under a hot shower again for as long as he could stand it, till he stopped shivering and screaming, stuff him full of hot food, issue him a crisp new uniform and clean boots-- and shove him back on a truck to the front, watched over by an armed guard. On the way, whenever the truck stopped, the men were not allowed to dismount, for fear they would desert. As any rational man would. Any man who valued life and did not count on Heaven.

"I did not want to go back in the line," Malpass said quietly, no hint of emotion in his voice. "Begged and pleaded. Bawled like a baby. Pissed my new clean pants." He laughed, bitterly. "Sat in the back of the truck and waited for a chance to jump out, to run away from the war, but a sergeant with dead eyes kept his tommy gun poked into my stomach, and I let them take me back." He paused and shook his head wearily. "God help me, I let them take me back."

Fr. Kellum knew what happened next. Now he knew the context. He had waited almost his whole life to hear it.

"When I got back in the line, there was this replacement padre forming up the men for mass, right there in the open. Insanity. I think they all knew what was about to happen." He snorted in disgust and resignation. "Probably welcomed it."

The first 88 came in and detonated in the treetops. Then a hail of 88s. The splintering trees whipsawed through the assembled men. "Human beings were coming apart before my eyes," he said very quietly. The chubby priest listened, his mouth open like a hooked trout. The seminarian looked pained, as if this were more than he had signed on for. The old priest went on: The din of the concussions blew out both his eardrums. At some point he dove into a hole and felt another man land on top of him.

And then time suspended. He went to sleep. His body shut down and his mind simply took him away from the carnage.

When he woke, it was dark and quiet and very cold. He was warmed by the body on top of him– the dead padre. Minus both his arms and the lower part of his jaw. He was soaked in the padre's blood, absolutely drenched in it. He wriggled out of the hole and lay on his side, trying to get a fix on the scene. In the moonlight it was almost beautiful– the ground dusted with new snow, the trees silvered against the glaze of moonlight, the branches of the trees hung with snow-dusted ornaments– but the ornaments were human remains, arms and legs and intestines, draped over the low branches. Twenty-seven men had simply evaporated.

"I went mad, I admit it," Malpass slowly said. "Then, all at once, I knew I was saved." How could this be true? It didn't have to be spoken by anybody. It was the ultimate test of faith. And it happened this way: He traded dogtags with the dead padre, simple as that. No thought, just instinct. Instantaneous reaction. Stole his collar tabs, rifled his pockets for a vial of holy oil and a purple stole and a rosary, left his own wallet in the padre's pocket, including the photograph of his wife and infant child, and left his life behind forever.

"So that is my sin," he said, head bowed but voice defiant. "I took Holy Orders from the pocket of a dead priest."

On the mantel an old clock ticked and outside new snow rattled against the lead windows. They all stared into the fire except Father Kellum.

"Tell the rest of it," Fr. Kellum said in a gentle voice but one which carried the authority of the Pope in Rome. And now the others, too, understood why he had come to Chicago in winter.

The old priest glared at him.

"You did it to escape the war, but it didn't work out that way."

"No," the old priest agreed, a strange bitterness in his voice. "I was cursed."

Fr. Kellum said, "You never left the line again, did you. You rescued the wounded. You heard their terrible confessions. You comforted the dying with Extreme Unction."

"That is my sin."

"For five months."

Yes, five months. Eternity."

"And then you didn't come home to your family."

"No, God have mercy."

The warm room had become suddenly cold, the others frozen, unable to speak.

"You stayed in Berlin." He did not need to say it all– Malpass' special gift for harboring the orphans of his enemy. The orphanages, the arrangements with wealthy families. How he saved a generation of kids. A priest who was not a priest, who had begun in a fit of madness..

"Tell the rest."

Fr. Malpass said, "Do what you came to do. I am an impostor. Tell me my penance." He slowly leaned forward in his chair until his knees were touching the rug and then he was fully on his knees, head bowed, before Fr. Kellum.

"Tell me your name."

Head still bowed, he said, "Private John Kellum, second squad, first platoon, C company, second battalion, Twenty-Eighth Division." He recited a serial number. Reached inside his cassock and yanked at the neck chain and his fingers came out holding a dogtag with the name Peter S. Malpass, SJ, and handed it to Fr. Kellum.

Fr. Kellum took it, then reached into his own pocket and pulled out a creased black-and-white photo of a young soldier in a class A uniform, barracks cap jauntily perched on his head. Next to him stood a young woman with wavy dark hair holding an infant in her arms. "The only letter you ever sent to my father," Fr. Kellum said.

The old priest took the photograph in his fingers and studied it, completely unmanned, as if he were dreaming in and out of his life. "My son."

"Died of cancer last year."

"And she–?"

"Years ago now."

"I never meant," he said. "I never meant."

"You know why I came."

"To take away my–"

"Absolution, grandfather," Fr. Kellum said.

Fr. Malpass looked up, baffled, his eyes aflame. A long moment passed. The seminarian crossed himself and stared at the fire, as if fiercely remembering a crippled kid's sledding party at a hilltop church all those years ago. "You cannot," Fr. Malpass said.

For there is something that inhabits men, he said in a strange voice not his own, an acid whisper of a voice, a voice from the madhouse talking to the ghosts of boys hanging in parts from shattered trees. And it is beautiful. And it is terrible. And it is in their eyes, and in their generals, who feed on the thing and make it great and release the great sacrifice of body and blood–"

He stared pop-eyed and worked his tongue over his dry lips.

"Now go on and tell the rest of your stories," he said. "Tell your story of the crippled boy who dreams of a Christmas sled, the lost farmer who finds his way through the woods and home to his family, the innocent woman in a strange land who yearns only for shelter and safety and a ripe manhood for her unborn only son."

Fr. Kellum lifted his right hand and blessed his grandfather with the sign of the cross, his fingers carving the air uselessly.

Day of the Dead: This Time

by Barry Silesky

Poised on the other side of
the space the body inhabits, brilliant,
fragile, like wildflowers, attached
to the end of a thread winding out,
is the only thing I want. A blink
amid debris, scent overcoming
factory, street, I can't see it,
drawing me closer as
it slips away. Is this the beginning?

If I want, a voice concedes, anonymous, certain. The first cold day of the season,
limbs drag flesh from chair to floor to chair, and I'm here. Holy music calms,
enchanting the background. But the same phrases keep repeating until I notice
the loop, a numbing hum in a room gone cold; and the charm
collapses: the body's analogue
closing the day.

There must be another song. Lover. Story. Words invoking the idea that must be
attended: the graceful, elaborate "toothache monster"-- lime green, orange,
blue, perched in the middle of the museum. Relatives' names to remember are
scrawled on bright colored scraps spread along a wall. Cartoon shapes decorate
another. Skeleton faces, bones in distorted shapes of human, black, with bright
primaries, fill a room. Low, curved shapes nearby say alive, though whatever
they were has gone wrong. A toaster, a gray necktie, a round wicker basket, a
cup, sit on the tables. But this is the only place they are, arranged to
commemorate the gone. We think we understand.

All the last weeks, David's father's been dying. Last week, it was Sharon's mother; Robin's a month before; Beth's is wheezing her last. Nerves fail the muscles,
and it takes an hour for me to get dressed, hoist up the body, fall into a chair. I

eat, drink, less than ever. But I've been here all day, and I'm hungry. Is this the way it ends?

A bright serpent, stretched out, twisted, leans five directions. Each end is a tendril, equipped with something vicious— talons, barbs, teeth. The danger's apparent and calls, calls, to clumps of passers who keep collecting to see.

Alone on a low pedestal on the other side of the entrance, a stone animal, thick, squat, rests as if sleeping. A reptile limb, bent, winds out from its trunk. Tonight it gets dark early. The clocks get set back. It's cold, and quiet. "Death of Myth" the stone is named. No one else was there.

A Fable with a Photograph of a Glass Mobile on the Wall

by Kevin Brockmeier

Once there was a cabinetmaker who had lived all his life in the same small town. There was a workshop along the western wall of his house, and in the afternoon, when the sun came pouring through the windows, he could be found there planing and turning and sanding pieces of walnut or cherry wood, coaxing himself along with phrases like "Take care it doesn't split along the grain" and "A little bit narrower at the base, I think." Eventually the light would become peculiar, its edges softening into shadow, and he would step back from his bench and survey the work he had done: a half-finished wardrobe or a dresser waiting to be stained. The bands of pale and dark wood seemed to pulse like waves in the fading light. When he heard the clink of silverware in the kitchen, he would give his equipment a quick wipe-down, wash the sawdust from his hands, and sit down to dinner with his wife and his boy.

The cabinetmaker enjoyed his trade so much that he rarely gave himself a day off. Sometimes, though, when the sky was gray and he could not make out the contours of the sun, he would put his boots on and take a long afternoon walk. There was a high school with a football field and a set of metal bleachers, a courthouse with a galvanized tin cupola, and a dance hall that stood empty in the middle of the week, haloed by gnats and moths, but that filled with music every weekend. Birds passed in and out of the hardwood forest on the far side of the meadow, and the stream that ran past the little stone church smelled like the snow from the fold of the mountains, a wonderful fresh smell of nothing living and nothing dying. The cabinetmaker's wife might come with him if the bank was closed, and his boy, too, if the schools were on holiday. A tremendous feeling of pride and satisfaction would wash over him whenever the three of them walked through the town together. It was the one place in the world where he truly felt familiar to himself.

The cabinetmaker had never considered himself an artist, only a craftsman, but as he approached middle age, he developed a richer intuitive sense of the woods he used: which knots would weaken a board and which would lend it distinction, how dark a particular piece would become after he applied the stain, how much a joint would expand and along which plane when the humidity rose. His reputation spread, and he began to take orders from other nearby communities and occasionally even from the big cities on the coast. He was a rarity, apparently— a joiner who did all his own work, using only local timber.

Then someone wrote a profile of his cabinetry for a magazine called Fine

Furniture, and suddenly everything changed.

It started with the letters, which began arriving a few days after the article was published, forwarded to him in bundles of twenty or thirty by the magazine's managing editor.

I recently read the feature story about you entitled "Artisan of the Sticks," and I was wondering do you also do sofas?

Do you have a web address? You really ought to have a web address.

We at Design Expressions wish to distribute your furniture directly to discriminating consumers from each of our more than one hundred stores nationwide.

Then came the second wave. Every afternoon, from the shelter of his workshop, the cabinetmaker was interrupted by dozens of phone calls from journalists and retailers, carpentry societies and parents looking for wedding gifts. It became harder and harder for him to find the time and the silence he needed to understand the wood he was trying to shape, the secrets it held in its rings and its fibers. It would not be long, he thought, before cars and minivans started nosing up to his yard, coughing blue smoke into the air and disgorging round after round of passengers.

One evening at dinner, listening to him complain about how little work he had gotten done that day, his wife said, "You know, you don't have to answer every single phone call that comes in."

But he *did* have to answer every single phone call: there was a conscientiousness about him that could not stand to ignore them.

"Well, then maybe you should think about taking a little break," she said as he sat stirring his peas together with his mashed potatoes. And although he had never before considered such a thing, the idea must have appealed to him, for a few days later, when he received a call from a small Northeastern college asking him if he would like to serve as a visiting professor in their woodworking program that fall, he surprised himself by accepting.

He had grown so accustomed to his town that it was hard for him to imagine living anywhere else, even for only a few months. What would he do without his wife and his son? he wondered. What would he do without his workshop, with its fine clear sunlight and its smell of walnut and cherry? And then there were the little things: the sight of the radio tower winking above the hills at night, the sound of the trees rattling after an ice storm, the rhythm of the automatic doors at the grocery store, the grasshoppers that sprang up from the fields like sparks from a bonfire—what would he do without those?

Yet he had agreed to take the job, and the day soon came when he had to say goodbye to his family, squeezing the back of his son's neck and tucking a lock of hair behind his wife's ear, and climb aboard the plane that would carry him to a city he had never seen before, a city of asphalt and washed yellow brick, so that he could move into the house he had arranged to sublet for the semester.

There is something innately sad about other people's homes. The rooms are crowded with the thousand-odd belongings that mark the presence of someone else's daily life: lamps and rugs, books and dishes, all of them gathered together and arranged in a process as slow and unthinking as the one by which a stream carves its way into the earth and then dries up. You can walk along the bed of such a stream, you can trace the tooling lines left by the current, but you will never taste so much as a single drop of water, and other people's homes present you with the same ornate sense of emptiness. This is never so obvious as when the people who live there have gone away.

The couple who owned the house where the cabinetmaker was staying were spending the fall in Italy, and their son had just left for his freshman year of college. The cabinetmaker felt as though he drifted over the floors of their home almost weightlessly, sleeping in their bed and drinking from their glasses without leaving behind the slightest trace of himself. He was always surprised when he found one of his fingerprints on the bathroom faucet or one of his stray hairs on the pillow. The Atlantic was only a few blocks away, and he could smell the salt in the air whenever he cracked open a window. Much of the furniture the couple owned was brushed steel and glass, though he was pleased to see that their two or three wood pieces—a dresser in the guest room, a sideboard in the dining room—were neatly constructed of Norway maple. The classes he taught were all in the morning, and on those afternoons when he would ordinarily have been shut away in his workshop with his thicknesser and his trying plane, he wandered around the house reflecting upon the various possessions he found. An oven timer in the shape of a pear. A hanging display of herb sachets. A ping-pong table with a lop-laced net.

Most of all there were the photographs that decorated the walls, small clusters of them in every room, capturing the child of the family at every phase of his life. Here he stood propped in the fork of a willow oak, tilting his head to look at the camera. There he occupied the stage in front of his high-school orchestra, grimacing slightly as he drew a bow across a cello. And over there he sat in a terry-cloth shirt with a frog and a bee stitched onto the front, dreamily poking his finger into his bellybutton.

Anyone could see how much his parents loved the boy, and as the cabinetmaker looked at the pictures, he thought with some small pensiveness of his own son, wondering how he was getting along with his new teacher and whether his wife had been able to convince him to give his bicycle another try.

The photos the cabinetmaker found the most puzzling were massed together in the front hallway: eighteen of them, of any subject or none at all, including a blurred image of somebody's sneaker, a closeup of a pretty girl in a woollen hat, a picture of what appeared to be the band of light along the bottom of a closed door, and a shot of a stained glass mobile made up of five red, blue, and yellow fish, taken from directly underneath. It looked as if someone had fired off the pictures without even bothering to glance through the eyepiece. There was no way the cabinetmaker could have known that this was exactly what had happened, that the images had all been captured by the same boy he could see perching in the willow oak and playing his cello, one on each of his eighteen birthdays, a tradition that began the day his parents left the camera in his crib and he accidentally released the shutter, taking the picture of the glass mobile.

Nor could he have known that while he was lying awake in bed at night, unable to fall asleep without the slowly swaying whisper of his wife's breathing beside him, the boy in the pictures was lying awake, too, staring at his dorm-room ceiling and wishing he was back home.

Nor, finally, could he have known that as he passed from one end of the house to the other, listening to his footsteps and gazing at the photographs on the walls, the photographs were gazing back at him.

It is no easy thing to wrest yourself away from a place where you have grown into your habits, and no matter how hard you try, some part of you is bound to remain behind. There was a fragment of the boy that had never left the house at all, just as there was a fragment of the cabinetmaker that was still tending the machines in the workshop and sitting down to dinner with sawdust all over his clothes. This fragment of the boy watched the cabinetmaker from out of the flat blue eyes of the photographs, following his movements with great curiosity. Why did he sleep so long in the morning? What did it mean when he laced his hands together and sighed through his nose? What did it mean when he started laughing, suddenly, out of a dead quiet? What did it mean when he took a pencil out of the jar, scraped a fleck of lacquer off the side, and held it up to the desk lamp for examination?

The boy in the pictures did not always understand the man, but the more he watched him, the more he grew to like him. Every day, for instance, in plain view of the photo magnets on the refrigerator, the cabinetmaker made a sandwich for himself out of luncheon meat and Swiss cheese, and every day his face gave a pucker of revulsion as he ate it. The boy in the superhero pajamas thought this expression of distaste was the funniest sight he had ever seen, the boy in the Cub Scout uniform showed a curling little smile as he looked on, and even the boy in the graduation gown found the phenomenon strange but somehow endearing: what was the story here? Was it the only sandwich the man knew how to make?

The boy in the framed portrait that stood on the desk in the study learned that he could listen to the cabinetmaker as he spoke on the phone at night. He said things like, "No, the classes are going fairly well, actually. I don't know how I'm doing it, but they really seem to be learning something," and, "That makes only the second call this week, doesn't it? It looks like all the fuss is finally dying down," and, "I'm just so exhausted by the end of the day," and, "I miss you, too, honey," and, "Give him a kiss from his dad, will you? And tell him he'd better not forget me." Afterward, when the cabinetmaker hunched over to rest his forehead on the desk, the boy wished he could reach out of the picture frame and pat him on the back, as his parents had always done for him whenever he had a bad day at school.

The boys on the wall of the family room, their faces dimmed by more than a decade of sunlight, watched the cabinetmaker from their swing sets and their bumper cars, eavesdropping as he practiced his lectures. They did not always follow the meaning of his words, but they liked the way he paced back and forth between the stereo and the television, flinging his hands around like someone conducting a symphony. "You can't just fit a few boards together and expect to have a lasting piece of furniture," he said. "You have to pay attention to the direction of the grain and the features of the particular wood you're using. Personally I've always felt that it's best to choose a wood that's native to the land-scape where you're working. Wood isn't like steel or plastic, after all. It comes from life, and even after you cut the roots and drain the sap, it continues to live in some way. It shrinks and expands with the seasons. It weighs more on a rainy day than it does on a dry one—did you know that? My point is that when you remove a piece of wood from the environment in which it has grown, it's much more likely to warp or to break on you."

The cascade of words came to a stop every so often as the cabinetmaker stood before the wall of photographs thinking through some idea that had occurred to him. Once, he reached out and brushed the cheek of the boy sitting behind the wheel of a tractor. The boy felt the touch as a soft wind blowing from the direction of the stables.

The cabinetmaker lived in the house for four months. The individual days seemed long and slow to pass, but the weeks went by more quickly than he would have imagined possible. The leaves turned colors, and the frost took the vines, and soon he was folding his clothes and finishing off the food he had bought and filling the giant filing cabinet in his head with the last time for this and the last time for that. It was the last time he would wash this glass. It was the last time he would empty this drawer. It was the last time he would open a window and breathe in the ocean air, with its great bold pinching smell of everything living and everything dying. The cabinetmaker had spent so many hours in the presence of the boy in the pictures that he barely noticed him anymore, but he could have seen him walking down the street at any stage of his life, and instantly he would have recognized him.

When he finally locked the door and slid the key under the mat, the boy was sorry to see him go. The house seemed bare and lifeless without him. A silence soaked into the rooms. The furniture stood peacefully in the shadows. The only sign of motion was inside the photographs on the walls, where the bow swept across the cello, the leaves of the willow oak shivered in the breeze, and the glass fish swam in leisurely circles through the air.

Elegy for a Limb

by Kenneth Pobo

On wet ground, a dead maple limb
I had meant to saw off for
months. A storm has taken him.
He looks stronger than before.
I slip on grass as I carry
him to the side of the house. He
takes my saw's bite with no
groan. I cut him into
segments. A hole, black as a crow,
shows how deep his wound went.
Bark hid his decline. Rot grew,
made no sound, gave no scent.
Trashmen will clatter on Monday—
toss him in, carry him away.

Escape to Olmstead Road

by Bonnie Jo Campbell

A few nights ago I was talking with Bob and Barb Lishin in their front yard. We were milling around, putting our hands in and out of our pockets, kicking hickory nuts into the driveway, watching our dogs roll on their backs in the leaves. Bob and I made jokes at the expense of Barb, who is fully nine months pregnant. We said that she really ought to get to raking those leaves.

As dusk turned dark, we retired to out respective homes. But a short time later, people with flashlights were wandering around our houses. Our dogs started barking, and Bob and I put on our coats and went into our respective front yards again. We found two tall, thin, poorly-shaven men dressed in white looking behind bushes and in our trucks.

"We's lookin'for a man who escaped from the nursing home," said the taller, thinner one, who was missing a front tooth.

"If he had the nerve to escape," I said, "he's probably all right." I'd like to think I'd escape too.

"Not in the head though" said the taller, thinner one, tapping on his own head. "He ain't okay in the head."

I shook my head as though I understood.

"Lady, you might want to go look in your garage if it ain't locked."

The shorter, fatter guy said, "Oh, he won't hurt you. He's a nice guy really. He's just nuts."

The beams of their flashlights danced across some raspberry bushes behind Bob's house. Cautiously I crept around in my garage and on my porch, jumpy at the prospect of actually coming upon the old man. Would he be crouching on the back porch behind my bicycle? Would I look out my bedroom window and see him grinning without teeth? Would he bite my leg if I tripped over him? Would he beg me not to call the nursing home?

Rain had threatened earlier but a warm wind had arisen with nightfall. There was only a sliver of a moon, revealed, obscured, and revealed again behind clouds,

Behind our houses were the woods and across the street was a big meadow. All around were places where a person could just decide that he wanted to go to be in nature, away from attendants and medications. Or where a fellow who was hungry might he could catch something to eat with his hands, a rabbit or raspberries. Or where a guy might sit and stare up at the moon and the clouds, or fold his hands behind his head and lie down.

I returned to my house, to my reclining chair beside the window, with my spotted dog at my feet. I drank a pot of weak tea by myself, watching the scattering of police cars, people with flashlights, neighbors. The ground in front of my house was covered with leaves which rattled in the wind, and crunched when people walked on them. Voices outside were indistinct.

Whenever I turned my head away, toward the kitchen where a bulb burned over the sink--the sink was full of pots and plates--I'd think I saw a flash of faded white from the corner of my eye. And I'd see my dog's left ear (he was lying in his right ear) point up as if he'd sensed movement.

But when I looked back to the window, there was only darkness and the dull sliver of a moon and the reflection in my window of the light burning over the kitchen sink. I couldn't even make out the leaves, or our rusting lawn furniture or the tall quiet grass across the road. So I just watched and listened expectantly, as though the window itself might become a figure in a thin white garment.

A few nights later, from this chair, I would see Bob and Barb in the driveway. Bob would carry a pale quilted bag and helped Barb into the truck before getting in himself. Bob would walk across my lawn and before he could knock on the door, I would have already opened it. "Michelle is asleep," said Bob. "Do you mind going over their until Barb's mom gets here?" I would say yes and watch their taillights disappear from their couch.

But on the night of the nursing home escape, I watched from my own chair. Surely, somewhere just out of my line of sight, there was a frail bone of a person, running soundless through the fallen leaves because he was almost weightless. His feet were bare (he must have lost his slippers). His eyes were free of his mind, and his downy hair was lighter than gravity and made his skull seem naked. The warmish wind whipped his gown all around, and he revealed as innocently as a baby that which a man Bob's age would carefully keep private.

Change the World
by Cris Mazza

1986

It was around then Home Depot opened less than a mile away. It was the first one Marcy had seen. Someday it would be torn down because it was too small. But back then, it was the most enormous hardware store anyone had ever imagined. Bigger than Handyman, than Builder's Emporium, than Dixieline Lumber. It went in where an old FedMart had been standing empty, so not everyone was worrying about big box stores accelerating sprawl, although Marcy voted for the no-development city councilmen.

After being married five years, Marcy and Kurt had bought a house. By changing little things in their lives and routine they'd been able to save the down-payment. She prepared meals from raw, fresh ingredients, and packed Kurt's lunch – cream cheese, walnuts and sprouts, or cheese, lettuce and tomato sandwiches – instead of him going out. She repainted the furniture she had in her apartment, the same stuff her mother had gotten from the Salvation Army 30 years ago. She and Kurt shared the 1979 sub-compact car Marcy had bought in the first year after graduating high school, and she put all of her bank teller salary into a money market account then just paid the bills with Kurt's paycheck. To stretch his salary, they also seldom went out to a concert or movie, never went on vacations, hadn't even had a honeymoon, except African nut soup at The Prophet, their favorite vegetarian restaurant – decorated with portraits of Mohamed, Confucius, the Dali Lama, the Maharishi, Rama, Lord Vishnu, even Jesus.

Their real estate agent had complained once that a client had looked too long at her legs instead of at the houses she was showing. Marcy giggled about that, later, to Kurt, because the woman had chalky-white legs the size of baseball bats. Still snickering, Marcy had speculated aloud whether the woman's sexy legs would help her make sales. Kurt merely suggested, "Maybe she knows how to use them." After closing escrow, the agent gave them a gift coupon from a home-improvement catalogue. Marcy said, "At least she's not offering you her legs," and chose a socket wrench set. Her father had never gone anywhere without his, and an extra one had always sat open on the coffee table.

On one side of their new house, the neighbor had a pile of rocks just about filling her back yard. The houses were built with their back yards against a little hill made of sandstone with smooth, globular rocks mixed in, as though this was close to the river, which it wasn't. Some freak of geology caused the hill to continually spill into the neighbor's backyard. Marcy planned to put iceplant groundcover on the embankment above her yard. Their piece of the hill wasn't falling, but it was bare, with hardened gullies of erosion.

The other neighbor had weedy grass a foot high, shaggy oleander bushes growing through a rusty chain link fence adjacent to Marcy's driveway, and a cinderblock wall separating the two backyards. But their street ran downhill, so that neighbor's back yard was higher than Marcy's, and the cinderblock wall that was over Marcy's head in her yard only came up to her neighbor's waist in his (just as the wall on the other side of the yard only came to Marcy's waist and she could look down into the yard full of rocks). The weedy-lawn neighbor also had a dog who put its front feet on the cinderblock wall and barked, with spit flying, every time Marcy went into her own back yard.

Kurt didn't notice these things because he didn't go into the yard. He practiced his Tai-chi and his electric keyboard and previewed promotional record albums inside the house. He was manager of a Wherehouse record store. So he was indoors the Saturday the police visited, after Marcy called them. Marcy had been in the yard trying to figure out what she should do about the places in the lawn that were just bare dirt because half the year they got no sun. (Sowing more seeds wouldn't do any good. She thought some sort of raised garden bed where she could grow vegetables, with park-like benches mounted on the timbers enclosing the garden.) The neighbor with the dog was actually watering his scrubby grass and disheveled bushes. He was also smoking and tossed his butt into Marcy's yard. Marcy retrieved it and went to the wall, holding the cigarette up toward the man as though passing a smoke up to a prisoner in a second floor cell.

"Please don't toss trash into my yard. This is still smoldering, it could've caused a fire."

"What?" the man replied. It looked like he might have no teeth.

She held the butt even higher. "Don't throw your cigarettes into my yard!"

The man turned, and his hose turned and squirted Marcy in the face.

The police, who arrived alarmingly quickly, spoke to the man, then knocked on Marcy's door. Kurt had to turn down Miles Davis or Chuck Mangione, Marcy couldn't tell them apart, although she did her Jazzercise to one of them.

"I don't think there'll be any more trouble, ma'am. He says it was an accident."

"He tossed a burning cigarette into our yard."

"He's just an old alkey," the other cop said. "We'll drive past a few times in the next half hour. He'll calm down."

"Alkey?" she'd asked Kurt, after the police left.

"Alcoholic." He was cleaning the record with special solution and a dust-free cloth. "Didn't he remind you of anyone?"

"Not particularly."

"Your father?"

"My father's not an alcoholic."

"Well, you should've called the police on your father, not our new neighbor."

"You didn't do anything."

"Do what? About what? Your father? I didn't even know you then." Kurt didn't look at her, slipping the record into its sleeve.

"No, you could've gone out and *said* something to ... the old alkey."

"Say what? About what?"

"He squirted me with the hose. It was no accident."

"So stay away from him." He pulled another record out of the stacked wooden grocery crates that exactly fit record albums. "Leave the yard alone, leave the grass alone, leave the hill alone, don't try to teach the neighbor manners. Why are you always trying to change everything?"

"To make things better."

"Better than what? Why can't things just be what they are? Why can't you just move into a house and live in it?"

"You mean don't fix anything?"

"Who's saying it needs fixing? Broken things need fixing. Leave everything else alone."

Marcy decided to put up a fence against the cinder blocks that would be high enough to block the dog and his owner from looking into her yard. 10-foot high fence boards would do it. Nail the fence boards, side by side, to two parallel 16-foot 2x4s – one 2x4 securing the fence boards at 3 feet from the bottom, the other 2x4 fastened 3 feet above that. Then stand the fence up flush against the cinderblock wall, and just pound 6-foot metal stakes into the ground on the other side to keep the board fence upright. After that, she would undertake the raised vegetable garden surrounded by picnic benches.

Her father never hit her, never laid a hand on her. He also didn't drink, no more than anyone else. He went to work, came home. He drove a cement truck for a while. Then other kinds of trucks. Gravel trucks, trucks delivering dirt here, picking up dirt from there. The things trucks did. If she still knew him, he could help pick up and deliver the railroad ties she would use to make the raised garden bed. But the last time she'd seen him was the day she'd arrived home from junior high and found her clothes, her shoes, her stuffed animals and caged rat all piled on the front lawn. Her dad had decided it was time for her to move in with her mother. If it hadn't happened, she wouldn't have met Kurt, because her mother lived a hundred miles away in Sacramento, with her new husband. It was too late to imagine her parents would ever get back together anyway, but someday her father surely would have to at least explain.

Kurt was three years older, a senior when Marcy started high school. He was in the band. Marcy was in the drill team that followed the band down the street, making crisp synchronized motions with white-gloved hands, the metal taps on the heels of their white boots clicking in unison. Their school mascot was a yellowjacket, so there wasn't much of a ready-made costume, except yellow and black. They'd worn tailored miniskirts, yellow with black inside the pleats. There was an alternate uniform that was black with yellow instead the pleats. But she hadn't really known Kurt then, just knew who he was because he was the band's president and marched with his trombone in the center of the front rank. She and Kurt didn't start dating until Marcy was a senior. Kurt came back for the homecoming football game. By then Marcy had quit her position as captain of the synchronized-hands marching unit and joined a boycott of the whole homecoming queen ritual. She was picketing outside the football stadium, carrying a sign that said *Cow Auction Today* and chanting *Hey-Hey, Ho-Ho, this big boob contest has got to go*. Kurt was in a little group of former band members who tried to drown them out with Sousa marches.

Apparently sparrows lived inside the Home Depot, it was that big. They flitted and chirped in the metal rafters overhead. Marcy was looking up as she wheeled a clunky lumber cart that never put all four wheels on the ground at the same time. She'd already loaded 24 ten-foot by eight-inch cedar fence boards and the two eight-foot 2x4s. As she was pausing over at the bins of nails, adding in her head, an employee passed, directing a customer farther down the aisle toward metal screws and bolts. The customer was someone Marcy knew. It was Colin, a boy from high school. Not just any boy, but her boyfriend in the 10th and 11th grades. She knew it was him even though this man was getting fat. His pants were too tight and he had a gut straining against a t-shirt over his overly-western belt buckle. His face was wide, his nose was broad, his head was enormous. His hair was considerably shorter than in 1978, and the blue on his face where he shaved was only on his chin and upper lip. In high school Colin had grown a fringe-like mustache, and Marcy had been glad when he'd had to shave it off for the 2-months of band competitions. He played the snare drum in marching band and tympani in the school orchestra, which replaced marching band as an elective in the spring. Colin had liked a girl who played cello as much as he liked Marcy, so he alternated between the two of them, for two years going with Marcy during band season, and the cello girl during orchestra season. In 11th grade, when the band and auxiliary marching units visited Disneyland after their last tournament of the year, Marcy had shoplifted a knit hat from a gift kiosk when Colin did; she thought if she didn't, it might be his excuse that year to break up with her so he could go with the cello player during orchestra season. At first Marcy was only choosing one of the longshoremen's hats because Colin was getting one. Then when she turned toward the cash register, he'd said, "Are you going to *pay* for it?" He'd balled his hat in his fist and turned to walk away, so she'd followed. They'd gotten caught. A grim plainclothes security guard led them to an office down a concealed alley off Disneyland's main street where they sat opposite a desk from another man, the shoplifted hats on the desktop along with some of the other junk they'd actually bought, like some sort of stuffed lizard from the Tiki Hut. The lizard stood on his mangled wire-manipulated feet with his mouth open and teeth showing, facing Marcy, and she just stared back at it, tears gushing, Colin hunched beside her, while the man reamed them and said he was calling their parents, but as far as Marcy knew he never did (unless he called her father by mistake). On the bus ride back to Sacramento, Colin and Marcy hadn't spoken. They'd sat crushed together in the back of the bus, Colin's hand in Marcy's shirt, rhythmically squeezing one breast, and Marcy still wept every now and then because she knew he would break up with her for the cello girl anyway, and he had, after not seeing Marcy at all during Christmas break.

It's not that Marcy thought about Colin once a week, even once a month, hardly even once a year in fact. But when she did, she had wondered if Colin would someday contact her and apologize for the shit he pulled in high school. Once when she'd mentioned that idea to Kurt, he'd laughed and said it would keep the post office and phone company in business indefinitely if everyone apologized to everyone they'd fucked over in high school. "Well, I would, if I'd jerked anyone around," Marcy had said.

"How about those girls trying to be homecoming queen?"

"My right to free speech."

"You threw mud on them."

"I did not!"

When he saw her, Colin said "Hi," but not a surprised haven't-seen-you-in-years *Hi*, just Hi. His smile didn't exactly exclude his eyes, but didn't include them either. Colin was half-Japanese and his almond eyes could be vacant when he stared dispassionately – like the times he broke up with her, or the time she didn't want to try his mother's seaweed-wrapped rice rolls – but she thought they had squinted merrily when he smiled, although she couldn't remember a specific time.

Colin's pants were too tight for him to put his hand in his pocket. He wedged his fingers in up to his knuckles, shifted his weight to one leg. Marcy was wearing overalls. She thought she might've had them since high school, but she could be remembering her painter pants, which she'd worn at a few school events, like the Earth Day rally, at which they'd chanted, *All we are sayyyying ... is give hemp a chance*, and carried signs that said *Hemp, not Trees*. They'd also spread dirt over part of the quad, to protest the paving of America. She'd loaned the stuffed lizard from Disneyland to a boy who had a sign that said *Ours to Protect, Not Destroy*.

Colin was wearing his inscrutable mask, the same face he wore the time he'd been absent from school on December 7, and when he came back the next day some boys started calling him Tojo. It was probably near the time Colin would be breaking up with Marcy after band season, so she hadn't said anything back to the kids who were ragging on him.

"So ... you building a ..." Colin examined her lumber cart, " ... paneling a room?"

"No, just a fence. A piece of a fence. Long story. I live near here, do you?"

"I moved to San Jose. But I own a rental house in Alta Valley. Needs some rain gutters."

"Wow, you own an extra house? It would've been weird if we'd ended up renting from you. We finally bought a house, Kurt and I. Kurt Carlson, remember him?"

"I don't know anyone from high school anymore."

"Me neither ... except Kurt, I guess. I didn't know him then. But you would know that. Hey ... whatever happened to, you know ... she played in the orchestra ...?"

Colin's expression, which maybe she was learning to read again, waited for more information before he finally shrugged. And as though giving in to someone pestering for a life story, he said, "I met my wife at work. When I was a security guard. Then I finished my associate degree and got a real estate license. I have three kids."

"Already?"

He didn't smile. He also didn't ask if she had any, so maybe it was obvious she didn't. The Earth Club in high school had some Zero Population Growth literature, and she'd mailed in a postage-paid card joining a mass-pledge not to have children. Before she got married, she'd been saving her money to get her tubes tied, but when she made the budget so they could save for a down payment, her savings all went into the house account. Not that it mattered that much anymore. Marcy and Kurt hadn't had sex in over a year. Sometimes she wondered if Kurt wondered what had happened to them, or what he thought about when he thought about it, or if he used Tai Chi to forget about it.

Colin cleared his throat, then said, "So ... did you ever become a lawyer?"

"A lawyer?"

"Didn't you want to be a lawyer?"

"When?" she laughed, "before or after my life in petty crime?"

"You're kidding."

"No, you know ... Disneyland ...?

What was on his face ... confusion? Marcy felt hot and looked up into the rafters. The sparrows were twittering contentedly. It had become part of the Home Depot white noise: forklifts beeping, paint-shaking machines ratcheting, shoppers droning, lumber carts groaning, squeaking, banging ... sparrows singing. A bird paused on a box of deadbolt locks on the top shelf of the aisle, in its beak a few bristles, perhaps from a broom or a paintbrush.

"Nesting." As Marcy spoke, the sparrow fluttered higher, into the roof beams. "Like us. We were going to change the world."

Colin was watching her, not exactly staring, but as though she was growing an extra eye and that's exactly what she was supposed to do, and what he expected.

"Well ... time to go make lunch for Kurt, or he might succumb to the smell of frying fat from the McDonald's on the corner. Want to come see my house and have a bite to eat?"

"No thanks. I've got some guys waiting to install gutters."

"Okay. You might not like radish sprout salad and miso bean soup anyway." She looked down at the box of nails she'd been holding all the while, remembering she only had peanut butter and cracked wheat bread at home.

Marcy had been a vegetarian since before going to live with her mother. Secretly at first, because her father still wanted beef or pork with every meal, and since 4th grade Marcy had cooked his dinners for him. But she'd taken a vow against meat when she was 12, the day her father squashed her new kitten under his truck tires in the driveway then took the mashed carcass and fed it to his dog. Kurt had been skeptical about the vegetarian diet at first, but curious, in that everything-you-do-is-interesting mood of a first date, which involved an Italian restaurant. By then she had also renounced white sugar, white flour and preservatives, which made an Italian restaurant difficult because of the pasta, but she could have the eggplant parmesan. Eventually Kurt had been easy to convert, especially after he discovered Tai chi.

"By the way, I like sushi now. Actually just the taki – rice rolls with vegetables, I don't eat fish. Like what your mother made, that time when I wouldn't eat it ...?"

"Did you meet my mother? I lived with my father and step mother."

"She was Japanese."

"So is my mother."

"But who made the taki – rice rolls – that time?"

"I don't know, what time?"

Colin didn't have a hand cart or shopping basket, just several packages of something in one hand. He started to move down the aisle, but slowly, not walking away from her. "Are you going to pay … ?" Marcy asked from behind, before she caught up. A clunk from the lumber cart before she could finish with the word now.

"Yeah, this's all I need. We started the job but were missing just a few bolts, so I ran over."

Marcy was trying to get the lopsided cart to roll not-too-unevenly as she walked beside Colin. He was going slowly, as though to accommodate her efforts, but he went into a 10-items-or-fewer line, so Marcy checked out at the next register, a little surprised to find him waiting for her when she was finished, an orange Home Depot bag balled up in his hand. He didn't grab a hold of Marcy's lumber cart, but again walked slowly beside it as she maneuvered out the sliding glass doors to the parking lot. Just outside the door an employee checked their receipts.

Marcy started to laugh, but when Colin's small eyes still just gazed like shiny opaque stones out of his overly large face, she said, "Am I going to be able to guess your car from the bumper stickers?"

It turned out his car was a station wagon with a *Baby On Board* sign suction-cupped to the rear window. The car next to his – one of those tiny old Hondas that several boys could pick up and move from the parking lot to the sidewalk in high school – had a *Nuke the Whales* sticker. After graduating from high school during the second oil crisis, when people lined up for blocks to buy gas, Marcy tried to go without a car. She'd already answered a roommate-needed ad in a weekly newspaper and moved in with a girl who turned out to be a born-again Christian. But the school Marcy went to that summer, to learn to be a bank teller, was across town from her new apartment and class started at 8 a.m., so she'd bought a used Datsun that promised 40 miles per gallon and made payments on it for a year. It was still their car – Kurt dropped her at work on his way – and her only bumper sticker was a fading *Carter/Mondale*. She and Kurt had been dating during the 1980 election, and Marcy had participated in door-to-door blitzes for the Carter campaign. She told Kurt if Reagan won, she was moving to a different country. On election day, she and Kurt were messing around on her bed with the radio playing an FM jazz station. She'd gotten off work at 4 and it was around 5, not really dark yet, just almost. Suddenly the radio was announcing Carter's concession. "No!" Marcy had yelped, vaulting off the bed, "wait for me!" Fortunately they weren't undressed yet. She and Kurt had run across the street to the VFW hall where the local polls were still open. When she remembers it, she thinks maybe they were both zipping their pants as they dashed into the voting booths. The next day, she'd dropped her purse into her drawer, slammed it with her shoe and announced, "Well, I'm moving to Canada." The other tellers looked up, most of them just airheads, bank robots – ATMs hadn't threatened anyone's job yet. That night when Marcy's roommate was playing her Christian quasi-rock in the living room, Marcy and Kurt huddled in her room and decided to get married and rent a house so they wouldn't have to share walls with anyone who might have that or any other unsavory taste in music.

"Well ...," Colin said.

"Yeah, nice running into you."

"Yeah, I gotta go."

Marcy was shoving her lumber cart up the parking lane, not very far away yet, and Colin called, "Hey ..." Marcy turned, bracing her weight to keep the cart from rolling back toward Colin. "I know why you were confused," he said. From that distance, his eyes were still just black spots, his face large and looking clammy, like he'd actually broken a sweat but hadn't noticed it yet. "My father got back together with my real mother. But wait, I think that was after high school. I can't remember. The only thing I cared about back then was not turning out like him."

After only a slight pause, Marcy said, "You did a good job."

Kurt had made his own peanut butter sandwich and went to his Tai-chi lesson in the park. His note said, "I can make it there in time on the bus, if I leave now." She thought he might call for her to pick him up, but they didn't have a cordless phone, and Marcy spent the afternoon making her fence, and luckily the spitty dog must have been locked inside. The hardest part was getting it to stand upright against the cinderblock wall by itself while she pounded the metal fence posts into the dirt. Also, the ground wasn't all that even, and in some places the bottoms of fence boards grinded into the dirt, at others they hovered above, not touching. Something about where the weight was distributed, and which part was absorbing the most pressure, was off, but it was standing there, blocking the neighbor from looking or spraying his hose or throwing anything into her yard, and blocking his dog from barking at Marcy.

Kurt had called and left a message saying he was going out after class with the instructor and few others. He didn't say so, but Marcy knew they went out for tea, not beer, and talked about chess and another game called Go.

If Kurt had been there when she'd gotten home, she would've said, breathlessly laughing, "Guess what I found out about my high school boyfriend!" If he'd come home while she was still hammering nails or setting the fence upright, she would've snickered, "I saw my ex-boyfriend at Home Depot and guess what, he's fat." If he came home now, as she sat in the living room sipping orange juice, she might have said, "I saw an old boyfriend in Home Depot today." She finished the juice and went to take a nap.

The sound that woke her was, at first, like a thunderstorm. A loud crack. A thump on the roof. Two more thumps. Another crack. Some of the other commotion was unspecific, and she could hear the old alkey neighbor's voice, but couldn't make out any words, as though he'd taken out his dentures and was having a fight with literal flapping gums. But an argument with who? His fleshy blousy wife who wore shapeless Hawaiian-print dresses, but who actually bothered to have a job? There was no second voice, but perhaps the other half of the argument was inside their house, and it was boomeranging back-and-forth to the outside, and the fallout was raining on the rest of the neighborhood. The front screen door bashed then shimmied for a second. More muffled thumps on the roof. Shattering of glass on concrete. Two, three, four more snap, crackle, pops. Bumps on the roof, and a vibrating, booming crash, like a gong, on the metal covering over Marcy's patio. Once during a halftime show, the band had played the 1812 Overture, and a special percussion section had been wheeled onto the field – huge base drum for the cannon blasts, a gong for the explosions, chimes for the church bells, while off the field someone had tried to time fireworks to detonate at the right place in the music. Now as she tried to hum the melody of the 1812 Overture, to fit with the racket outside, Marcy remembered she had slipped a black glove over one white one, then raised her fist and left the football field in protest over the glorifying of war for entertainment, although the Earth Club had voted not to stage a demonstration that night since they needed to get student government money for their rain forest float in the homecoming parade. (After Marcy walked off the field, the faculty leader of the drill team had told her she was being replaced and suspended for a week, but Marcy decided that when she walked off, she had also, right then, quit her position as captain.)

Everything became quiet, and Marcy was counting inside her head. She got to a hundred, then two hundred, and it was still quiet. But she closed her eyes, waiting for more. The war in Vietnam had been over by the time Marcy got to high school, and not a single boy she knew would be drafted or go overseas to a battlefield, but she was thinking about Vietnamese villagers caught in the crossfire between Vietcong and American forces, hiding in their huts, counting the seconds between burst of shelling. But then again, the village was never just caught in an unfortunately located battle; the village was the battle, the village was the target.

Marcy padded in her socks through the living room, into the kitchen. Through the kitchen door window she saw a brown beer bottle in three pieces on her concrete patio. Two more brown bottles, whole, on the dirt in the yard that should be growing grass. Then, off to the side closer to the alkey neighbor, she saw a broken piece of wood ... then another, then another. Her whole fence was smashed, many of the upright cedar fence boards splintered off and tossed into her yard. The rest, a jagged snarl of fractured boards twisted askew but still attached to the 2x4, lying flat, with more broken bottles glinting among the kindling.

Marcy backed up, squatted on the kitchen floor, breathing hard but not crying. If she could've called Kurt, she would've. But this was before cell phones, before pagers. Long before e-mail and chat rooms and instant messaging. Before Columbine and Oklahoma City and OJ. She crawled back to the bedroom, shut the door and turned off the light, started a fan to create white noise, to drown out anything else she might've heard. And without sleeping, managed to not even hear Kurt come home until he flung open the bedroom door, demanding, "What the hell's going on? There's dogshit by the front door. Someone threw dogshit at the house."

"Dogshit *too*?" Marcy whispered.

"Yeah, it's all over the driveway."

"It's more than that," Marcy said softly, without moving, without turning toward Kurt. "The neighbor, he broke the fence I made, he threw bottles and trash into the yard. He went on some sort of rampage."

"You had to go and stick up a *fence*?"

"I told you why."

"Yeah, and *now's* when we should be calling the police, but we can't – he did this *because* you called the police."

"I was only trying to give us some privacy in our own yard."

"I don't go in the yard. I don't care about the yard. How about what happens here, in *here*? How come you're not obsessed with fixing what happens, or doesn't happen, in *here*?"

Marcy rolled to her back and looked at Kurt. He was very thin, had always been thin. He had narrow shoulders and a lean face. Once at a bank party, when someone said he was lucky he could eat whatever he wanted and not gain weight, someone else teasingly asked him if he'd been a POW. The two people had both been women.

"Please, Kurt, could you go pick it all up? I can't bear to look at it. Please ...?"

Kurt left, and over the fan Marcy didn't hear anything. Until, after a while, she heard the refrigerator open and close. She heard the mumble of the television on the other side of the wall. On Saturday at five there were reruns of Kung Fu.

Grasshopper still wandered around the old West, spreading quiet wisdom, having women fall in love with his unflappable self, never succumbing to temptation, although she had wondered aloud to Kurt once, snickering, whether he boffed every one of them, but it just wasn't part of the storyline.

When Marcy came out to make something for supper, she peeked into the yard and didn't see any debris.

"What did you do with the dogshit?"

"Trash."

"What do you want for dinner?"

"Some of that dogshit sounds good."

"Want to just get burritos from the place on the corner?"

"I thought they had lard."

"Can't be any worse than dogshit."

The following week, on Saturday afternoon while Kurt was at Tai chi, Marcy was taking a bag of indoor trash to the cans on the driveway, and the old alkey neighbor was in his front yard, again with a hose. Her trashcans were around the side of the house nearest his. The bags of beer bottles and dogshit had departed with the trash pickup that week. Curbside recycling wouldn't begin for another year or two, so the beer bottles had gone into the regular trash. Ordinarily Marcy would have insisted they keep the bottles and pieces of bottles separate and drive them over to the recycling center near the landfill, but she didn't say a word when the glass had clinked like chimes inside the bags as she carried them to the curb. The stack of splintered fence boards had been too much for one pick-up and was still on the side of the house beside the cans, waiting to go into the trash little-by-little.

Marcy put her head down and started to skitter around the side of the house, but the neighbor called out, "Hey ... hey c'mere." Without his dentures again, his words as spitty as the dog's bark over the backyard cinderblock wall. Marcy looked up. The man gestured for her to come closer. He was wearing one of those pleated-down-the-front shirts, like a dentist smock. His salt-and-pepper hair was thick and longish, but lank and stringy. Marcy was coming nearer as slowly as she could. He gestured again, then dropped his hose. "C'mere, I want to show you something." Every 'S' blew out some spit. Kurt had warned her not to antagonize him again. "Come around the fence," he said, so she did, coming around on the sidewalk to his front yard, and when she got there he was holding a shovel.

"I got something I want to give you," he said. "I'm so ashamed for what I did. I got something to give you."

"You don't have to give me anything."

"What I did was terrible, I want to give you something."

As he spoke, he was going around the side of his house, on the other side of the same cinderblock wall where Marcy had put her fence, but here it only came to her waist. She stopped to see how her yard looked from up here. It was a fairly complete view of everything: everything she'd planned to fix but hadn't yet, the dirt where grass should be, the bare embankment that could come sliding down, and the top side of the metal roof over the patio where she saw a faded green fris-bee and a deflated rubber ball that looked like a stomach. There were also four more brown bottles, several fist-sized rocks, and some grayish looking things that were obviously turds.

"Look there," the man said. Marcy turned away from the startling view of her own yard. The man was pointing with his shovel to the dirt beside the foundation of his house. A skinny rubbery plant was growing all alone there, with a few thick leaves and a long neck supporting one dark bruise-colored flower. "It's a black lily," he said. "They're very rare. You dig it up and take it to your yard."

"You don't have to give me this."

"Take it, because I did such a bad thing. I know I did a bad thing."

Marcy stared at the lily because she didn't want to look at the man's toothless mouth or the sweat starting to ooze from his hairline. She groped for the shov-el and he put it into her hand. The dirt was hard, but she managed to get most of the shovel under the lily, in a circle all the way around, until the lily with its roots in a dirt-clod were on the shovel, and she carried it home that way, then passed the shovel up to the man over the cinderblock wall. She dug a hole right there, beside the cinderblocks and planted the black lily. Its neck was flaccid and the flower sagged to the ground.

Marcy never built the raised garden surrounded by picnic benches. She did put flagstones down where the lawn was mud, and she put a flower trellis up against the cinderblock wall, with a fast-growing jasmine to block the neighbor and his barking dog. But the neighbor shot his dog one night, the sound of the gun making Marcy bolt upright in bed while Kurt never stirred. Later that year she would sit naked in a hot tub – at a former downtown motel remodeled to rent out dayrooms with saunas and Jacuzzis – beside a supervisor from the bank. She kept washing her mouth out with the chlorinated water between the times she went down on him, because there wasn't a lot of information on whether oral sex was safe. She wanted to be promoted from teller. The follow-ing spring she was living in an apartment, alone, and the house had a *For Sale* sign when the black lily would have been sprouting again. On her last trip moving the last of her stuff, which Kurt had packed and left on the porch for her, she went into the house to leave a note for him. She didn't know what the note would say. She eventually left without writing it, but before that, she went through the kitchen and out to the yard to check the dirt beside the cinderblock wall for any sign of the black lily.

Things One Does Not Regret

by David Mura

In Osaki Marsh the wild duck flaps its wings,
trying to shake the frost settled on its tail
--the lines remind her of the plover's cry
on Sao river, vanishing in the misty banks,
as she writes by candles a thousand years ago,
and all I can think of is what she looked like
and how I might have appeared to her
in the gowns of a Chamberlain
of the Fifth rank, bearing sweet chestnuts
for the Great Council banquet. Oh
she was like a rosary of rock crystals
or plum blossoms blanched with snow;
a pretty child eating strawberries: That's
how someone who didn't live then
still sees her. But I, I know
she didn't simply love the *hotogisu*
alone, but anything that cries in the night
delighted her—except babies, except babies.
(Yes, even the hawkings of jealous wraiths.)
If I was the basket worm at the bottom,
I was begotten by a demon, forgotten
by my mother, and I grew beyond my father's
frightening nature, abandoned as I was,
abandoned as she became with me
which made her sorry ever after.
And so I sit here, watching the ants skim
across the surface of the water. Then sinking.

The hostage husband

by E. Ethelbert Miller

You wake not knowing
Which group of insurgents are holding you hostage
You've been wearing a blindfold since the first day of marriage

Circus Animal

by E. Ethelbert Miller

Another day
Inside this cage

My life broken
Into so many pieces

I keep cutting myself
Against the bars

Untitled

by G.W. Clift

A lone I stood at my twenty-eighth floor window, looking down. The window didn't open, and that made up my mind. Or made making up my mind a moot point.

That must have been around coffee break time, because when I left my office, the halls were full of office workers heading for the elevators or stairs, for their break rooms or to visit friends someplace else in the thirty story building. I was going down to the ground floor lobby to buy a paper. I wanted to find something to read, something about something important.

The main bank of elevators were so busy that potential riders stood, seven or eight deep in the marble-floored hallway, around the closed metal doors. I paused to brush the hem of my tweed skirt flat and then walked on, making for the other elevators, the ones in the back of the building, elevators which a lot of people didn't even know were there.

Soon I was alone in one of the hallways, or alone except for a young man walking along just behind me and off to my left. He was right on my pace. I turned to look at him.

He looked up. "Sorry," he said, and he went on by me toward the back elevators. He had on rubber-soled wingtips. As he walked on, he took off his top coat and reversed it, as if he was expecting rain outside and wanted to get the waterproof side out. But I wasn't really watching him. I knew the route I was taking and simply followed the corridor. So I didn't need to be looking up at all. He went from generally gray to generally khaki there in my peripheral vision

"Hey," I said. "Hold the door."

He sprang forward just in time to stick his arm in the closing elevator door.

"Is this going to be faster than the stairs?" he asked me as the door began to open again.

So I looked up at him. He was a little shy of six feet tall, about a hundred and fifty pounds, with about an inch of hair all over his head, and a pair of wire-rimmed glasses. I'd say he was younger than me by three or four years, and I was thirty-two.

"Oh yeah," I said. "At least, I expect it is." Then he and I got onto the elevator and the door closed behind us.

There were a couple of older men in dark suits already in the car, deep in conversation. They got off three floors down taking the smell of pipe tobacco with them.

"I can't believe the elevator isn't packed with people," the young man in the top coat said.

I shrugged. "Somebody else will get on before long."

He was looking down at his shoes. "You work up at Larson's?"

"Daycraft," I said. "We've got a suite up on twenty-eight besides the whole of ten and eleven. My department is just down the hallway from Larson's, though."

"Oh," he said, nodding his head. His eyes were hazel.

"You were doing something at Larson's?"

He shook his head and looked down again. "Damn. I'm in for it."

Then we stopped at fourteen and a couple of middle-aged women got in. One of them was wearing gloves. "Six, Deborah," she said to her companion, who then had to step around me to light that button with an index finger.

I wondered about what he was worried about, but he didn't speak as we descended. He kept his eyes on the floor. And he took off his glasses and put them in his coat pocket.

The women got out on six. Then, at the ground floor, the young man with the coat and I stepped off the elevator together, and we were with each other when I heard the sirens approaching. When we rounded a corner in the corridor, he looked toward the street door. He brushed his hair back with both hands.

"I hope you won't mind," he said to me. "I hope you won't mind if I treat you like a friend. I need one just now. If the police stop us, I may say that we've been together for the last hour. Would you please not contradict me on that? You don't have to say you know me or anything--just that we've been in sight of each other."

"What did you do?" I asked.

Then he turned to look at me and I saw he was nervous. But he looked right at me. "I didn't do anything. Honest."

Half a dozen policemen came in at the street door. They spread out, going down different hallways. Two took up places at the door. The top coat-wearing young man and I kept walking. When we came up to the policemen guarding the exit, one of them spoke to us.

"Hi," said the younger of the two cops. "Did you two just come down one of those back elevators?"

I nodded.

"Did you see a guy in a gray top coat?" the cop asked. "Did a guy in a gray top coat come down in the elevator with you?"

"A couple of women," my companion said. "That's it."

"What's up?" I asked the cop.

"Did you see a guy in a gray overcoat? He may have discarded the coat, of course, but we don't know what he would have been wearing underneath it."

"We haven't seen anybody else," I said. "Two older men got off on twenty-five, I think it was. And the women got off at six." But the policeman wasn't even listening to me at the end. He was listening to the radio on his belt.

"Did they say 'Princeton' or 'Winston'?" the younger cop asked his partner. We walked by as they were talking this over.

Once we were outside, I folded my arms against the autumn cold.

"Thanks," my friend from the elevator said. He seemed shaken. "Really, thanks a lot. Would you mind holding this envelope for me for a couple of days? Somebody will ask you for it—somebody who isn't the police. Please don't lose it. If you have any trouble because of the envelope or because of what we just told the cops, check with One Two." And he turned quickly and walked off and around a corner, across the street, and out of sight.

I had no idea what he meant by "One Two." And I didn't know what any of the fuss with the police was about. I turned the plain, white, number ten envelope over once. Its flap was tucked in. On the front someone using some sort of fountain pen had written the word "Control III." I held the envelope tight and walked out into the sunlight and around to the front of the building, thinking I'd get my newspaper.

There was quite a crowd around the building's main entrance. Uniformed police stood at the doors, asking questions of anyone who tried to get in.

"Miss," said the short officer at the door. He had a uni-brow and made a face as if he'd just eaten something really acid. "Do you have a reason for wanting to enter the building?"

"Yes," I answered. "Why do you ask?"

"There's been some sort of trouble upstairs. We're just keeping people out who don't have any real reason for going in, at least until they get the alarm off and figure out what the trouble is."

"You've got the building surrounded because somebody tripped the alarm? Never mind. I work for Daycraft Corporation, in the Human Services office, in this building. So I'm simply going back to work," I told the little cop.

He let me in. Carrying the envelope right out in plain sight, I walked past a dozen or so other cops on my way to the newsstand. There I bought a Morning *Prospect-Journal*. The cops weren't letting anybody onto any of the elevators, front or rear, so I had to walk up the stairs. On the third floor I took an elevator on up to my office.

On my floor there seemed to be a lot of people out in the corridors. But I didn't see any police.

"Tell me what's up," insisted Deidre, the new secretary I shared with Jason, myopic Terry, and the woman whose name may have been Babs.

I shook my head.

"Something happened over at Larson Inc.," she said, a little excited. "The office manager came running by here half an hour ago, asking if I'd seen a strange man in a gray overcoat. And at first I thought she was kidding, that it was a flasher joke. But she wasn't smiling. And a few minutes later Terry saw policemen walk into the Larson offices. Since then everything's been stirred up. Margaret has the t.v. on to see if there's any news."

I went into my office and took out a new envelope. I wrote my own name and the address of a friend's restaurant on the outside. I considered opening the envelope I'd been given to hold, but decided I didn't really care what was in it. So then I put the "Control III" envelope inside the new one. I sealed my envelope and took it out to the mail room and ran it through the meter. Then I slipped it down the glass mail drop in the wall between a couple of elevators.

When I got back to my office, the phone rang. It was Richard, my husband.

"Your office building is on the news," he told me.

"Really? What for?"

"The reporters don't know. There are lots of police in and around the building. Apparently they are looking for a man who may be in there with you."

"With me?"

"You know what I mean. This joker may still be in the building. Nothing much shaking that you can see?"

"No," I said. "You know how it is with news reports. All noise. Are you at home?"

"I'm in the office at the plant. Break time. What's for dinner tonight?"

"I better get back to work. Goodbye, Richard."

I walked into Brendan's office. Brendan Finney was the new department chief.

"Hello, sweetheart," he said to me. "The police think they have some man trapped in the building who took something from Larson's. Apparently it was something important." Brendan opened a cabinet door and turned on the t.v. inside. Then he reached over and stroked my hair.

"Who cares?" I said. "No. Leave the t.v. on. The noise'll cover..." I gave him a kiss.

We made out a little there in his office. Brendan left the priesthood after he was forty, so he wasn't quite as sexually experienced as he should have been at his age. Sometimes during that brief and casual affair, his inexperience made things a bore for me. He rarely initiated anything. And he complained that I acted on impulse too much.

Eventually I quit kissing him back. He looked up at the t.v. and asked me what I thought about all of this--two white police helicopters circling the building and people being stopped coming in and going out.

"I don't think anything about it," I told him, straightening my blouse.

Then the police burst into the office.

"What is this?" Brendan asked, getting up off the carpet.

"Are you Melinda Ashford?" one of the policemen asked me.

"Yes," I admitted.

They handcuffed me and took me away. We rode an elevator down to the lobby.

They put me in the back of a van that didn't have windows and drove me to some sort of government building and immediately put me in an interrogation room. When a man and a woman in shirt sleeves came in, I told them I wanted to call my lawyer.

"That won't be necessary," the woman told me. "You aren't under arrest. We just asked the officers to bring you here so you could tell us about the man you rode down the elevator with about ten this morning."

I thought for a second. "I went downstairs to get a paper during my break. That's the only time I was in an elevator after my arrival at the office."

"Yes," said the woman. "We want to know about the man who rode down with you."

"There were several other people who got on and off. I didn't know any of them."

"You rode down with one man."

"Did I? I don't remember him. There were a couple of older guys in gray suits that got off a couple of floors down from where I got on, I think."

"This was one guy. By himself."

"I didn't know anybody on the elevator. That's usually the way it is in such a big building. Although I sometimes recognize people I've seen around." The cops who had come into the building as we were leaving didn't see me on the elevator with the envelope guy--with Top Coat. So it must have been the two older men or the two women who got on at fourteen who told these investigators about me and the guy with the "Control III" envelope. Unless the elevator had a secret camera in it.

"I don't think we've made ourselves clear to you," said the male interrogator. He stood up, and he was like six foot six. "We want to know about the man who rode down the elevator with you during your break this morning. The one guy who was alone except for you."

I shook my head. "I must not have been paying attention. Did he have something to do with the security alarm and all the policemen at the building's street doors? Can I go to the bathroom? Please?"

They left me alone for an hour in there. It was cold, and I needed to go to the bathroom. Then they came back and asked me if I'd remembered the guy they wanted to hear about. I told them I thought everybody who came into the elevator car came in as a component of a pair. So then we all sat quietly for another hour. Then they let me go to the bathroom.

I spent the night in a cell, alone. They fed me once. The food wasn't very good, but I ate most of what I was offered. Then they asked me questions three times before what must have been about midnight of the second day of my interrogation. I couldn't ever see any clocks (they'd taken away my watch) or windows, so it was hard to know what time of day it was. Then they brought me into the interrogation room again.

This time they kept asking me questions, first about the guy in the elevator and then about my job and about what I knew about the other businesses with offices on that floor and about what foreign countries I'd visited and about where I stood on the Armenian controversy and whether I believed Lee Harvey Oswald acted alone and so on. They apparently wanted to keep me up all night. But they were both yawning after a couple of hours. Finally they went away for a little while. Then they came back, each of them carrying a cup of coffee, and we started again. Eventually the man fell asleep with his head supported by a hand supported by an elbow on the table. And then the woman had to go out. I waited a couple of counts and then went out after her. My watch was clamped to a clipboard which was hanging from a hook right beside the door. I took the watch back. Then I walked through the empty corridors. I kept walking away from sounds of human voices and activity. Pretty soon I found a stairwell and went down to the ground floor and out a back door. Then I walked down hill, along a series of residential back streets, until I found a creek. And I walked downhill along it, ducking branches and stepping over trash until I got to the river, where the going was a little easier. I walked in the direction the water was flowing until I recognized the part of town I was in. It took me an hour and a half to walk home from there. It was the middle of the night, and the streets were almost empty.

I got into the apartment building by swiping my security card through the reader. It took another swipe to get into one of the elevators. Up I went to the twenty-third floor. When I got to the apartment, I shut the door to the bedroom so that I wouldn't disturb Richard. I turned on the Schoenberg at a very low volume, and I took a long bath and changed clothes. I was careful not to break the yokes as I dropped two eggs into the frying pan, I looked at them for a moment, and then I scrambled the two eggs in the skillet and made toast, cut off the crusts, and smeared what was left of the bread with raspberry jelly. Then I ate the crusts.

At about seven I started walking toward work--my car was still in a parking building near the office.

When I got to the office building I bought a paper in the main lobby newsstand, partly so I'd know what day of the week it was. Turns out it was Thursday. There was a story--not a very big story--about security concerns at downtown offices. I read that on my way up in one of the elevators.

When I got up there I asked Deidre, who was playing Minesweeper on her computer, if she'd seen Brendan. "Haven't," she said. "But, then, you knew he was asked to leave yesterday. Didn't you?"

"Fired?" I asked.

She made a face as if she hadn't heard me.

"Canned? Released?" I suggested. "Cashiered?"

"Separated. Axed. Sacked," she said. "You know-- 'asked to leave.'"

"And he complied with the request?" I asked.

"Sure," she said, as if surprised I'd even ask.

I went into my office. I sat down. I paced, thinking hard. I went to my office phone, pushed the speed dial button, and hit one and two.

At the other end a phone rang. Then a sleepy sounding woman's voice answered. "Trouble?" she asked.

"I don't know what to do with the--you know."

There was a pause. "Well if its just that, why wake me up? Oh, well. Let me look at my notes. I see it. If you'd like to go see the future on Wyndham Street today, that would be fine. But make it later, rather than earlier, won't you? Give a girl a break."

I had lunch at David's Indonesian restaurant. While I was eating rice table, he brought me an envelope addressed to me that had been delivered to the restaurant the previous day. We talked about films for a little bit. He'd gone to see a long war epic the night before, and the print had broken twice during the first hour. So then he'd gotten to auditorium hopping. He'd seen bits of five other movies, watching as much as twenty minutes of each one before moving on. Not that he seemed to have enjoyed himself. Eventually he realized there was an usher going from auditorium to auditorium with him and sitting down to watch each film until David got tired and moved on. The usher didn't tell him to quit hopping. He didn't even speak to him. But it creeped David out that this polyester-clad hell hound was on his trail, so he left the theater and spent the rest of the evening doing sport dumpster diving, though he didn't find anything worth keeping.

After lunch I went to the art museum there on Wyndham Street. The museum was pretty much empty of people, particularly when I got into the Futurist gallery. I didn't even see a guard in that suite of rooms. I sat down on a bench in the middle of a long gallery from which I had a clear view of an irritating Boccioni painting.

Forty-five minutes later a big, roan horse of a woman of maybe fifty-five came into the room, slapping her huge feet down in front of her as she came.

"Hello," she said to me. "Do you have anything for me?"

"Why would I?"

"That I don't completely understand. But it is my observation that people generally do what they're asked. And you were asked to do a favor for a man--to hold something for him until it was called for. Isn't this as you remember it?"

"What am I supposedly holding?"

"An envelope," she said.

"What's in it?" I asked.

"I don't know. Why don't we take a look?"

I pulled the "Control III" envelope out of my coat pocket. It was inside the envelope I'd addressed to myself at David's restaurant. The big woman sat down on the bench beside me. I opened the outside envelope and put it in my pocket again. That left the envelope I'd been given by the guy on the elevator. I looked at my companion and then lifted the flap.

Inside was a love note written in purple ink on that scented sort of paper that girls get from their aunts for their fourteenth birthdays, the kind with a butterfly fixed in one corner of each sheet. The paper was lilac. And the message, written in a florid cursive, said:

May 8,

Rum-tum Kitty--

I can't get free this afternoon. And I'm so, so sorry. But there will always be other days, forever and forever, yours,

Saucers

This irritated me.

"What does this mean to you?" I asked the horse woman.

"Nothing," she said, shaking her head. "I think the guy must have grabbed the wrong letter." She stood up. "Oh, well. Guess I'd better be going. Nice to meet you." She walked out of the gallery making an echoing noise each time she put a big foot down.

After a few minutes I wadded up the letter and the envelope that said "Control III" on it. I stuffed that trash in a receptacle in the gallery shop and wandered back out to the street.

There I saw a yellow school bus. A class of elementary school kids were getting off.

"We're going into the museum," one of them told me. "We're going to look at Art History: The Last Dozen Years."

Other kids were nodding.

"Are you? That might be kind of interesting," I said. "I wonder if your teacher would mind if I went along."

The little boy shrugged his shoulders. "Just be sure to ask 'please.' "

That night, as I sat alone in the window seat in the apartment, looking out onto a gentle rainstorm, I fantasized that the guy in the elevator and I were talking about something. We were sitting in a park, in the sunlight. And what we were talking about seemed very important. We both laughed and gestured as we talked, and we promised to devote our lives from then on to that one idea. Whatever it was.

* * *

Wind Thinks

by Kenneth Pobo

only of force--
the screen only
of resistance,

lucky for the plastic table
which no longer tips over,
unlucky for wind

chimes craving a push
that never comes.

Letter To Laura

by Elizabeth Searle

Dear Laura Bush:

Your hands are so cold.

This is what you told my mother. This was in 2000, in Phoenix, on a campaign visit to an icily air-conditioned private school. So your own hands, though you seemed not to know it, were cold too. My mother was school Librarian, looking forward to meeting you because you had been a Librarian too. Among the students in my mom's posh school were children of Senator John McCain. Your husband's campaign, of course, used McCain's adopted child to try to convince voters down South that McCain had an 'illegitimate black child.' Of all such dirty tricks, surely, your hands were clean.

Clean but-- like my mother's hands when you two shook-- cold.

Your hands are so cold, you told my mother. Which prompted my Mom to tell me, when I asked what she thought of famously perky wanna-be First Lady Laura Bush: She's not like what you see on TV; she's a cold fish.

It's not like what you see on TV, you said in your husband's defense the week after Katrina as you visited a carefully selected well-maintained flood shelter in Mississippi. The people there were not swamped by their own sewage like those in the New Orleans Convention Center, not packed together like the flood victims in the Houston Astrodome whom your mother-in-law claimed were so much 'better off' this way. The victims you visited certainly weren't dead or dying on airport luggage conveyor belts like the 'worst-off' victims in the makeshift New Orleans airport terminal hospital that your husband-- holding a press conference on the runway-- refused to see.

Once, years ago, you didn't see a Stop Sign.

You crashed your '63 Chevy into a '62 Corvair, killing a boy you'd longed to date. You were a Senior at Robert E. Lee High School; your victim was DOA at Midland County hospital; you, I read with some sympathy, 'couldn't bring yourself' to attend the funeral. An interviewer in 2000 asked how it felt to be asked about that long-ago crash, to be reminded of it. You replied, coolly, that you were reminded of it even when you weren't asked, every day.

I liked you for saying that.

I liked you for saying, back when you'd had trouble conceiving a baby, that you started avoiding the baby aisle in the supermarket.

I liked you for saying, when asked in the early years of your marriage what it was you did: I read. Later when you were married you ammended this to: I read, I smoke, I admire. I can relate; my friends and I.

We read; we smoke or drink; we criticize. Sometimes we criticize your husband, sometimes as mindlessly as you'admire' him. Like many of my friends, I hate your husband so much, am so repelled by him on every level, I can barely bring myself to watch him, listen to him. As he was being inaugurated, I cancelled my New York Times subscription. Like that'd show him. Like anything-- even this-- will show him.

Is it true, Laura, you take Prozac? You and your husband do share an air of unnatural, unearned, how else to explain but chemically enhanced serenity.

You're doing a heck of a job, Brownie, your husband told the now-infamous FEMA Head he'd appointed. My 6 year old son asked: What would NOT a 'heck of a job' look like?

Poor scapegoat 'Brownie': a man with a nickname like the names of the rich men's horses he'd coddled in the job he lost shortly before being handed the slightly larger responsibility of holding whole human lives in his hands.

I used to work for a Human Services Temp. agency called something like: Helping Hands. At the time I was a Writing Grad. student, an ex-babysitter, ex-Santa's Helper and ex- movie theater Popcorn Girl. Like Brownie, I know something about taking on a serious job you are unprepared for, one that turns out to be more than you can handle. Once amidst a near hurricane-strength storm, I was assigned as the sole Emergency 'Sub' for overnight at a Group Home for Mildly Retarded Adults.

All the electricity in the Home went out in the storm. The cold house was filled with moans. Haplessly, I shone a shaky flashlight on the slick pages of a book the Home kept on display called WHAT TO DO IN AN EMERGENCY.

I stared dumbly at the RAPID ACTION GUIDE, WHEN SECONDS COUNT, at the sketches of various victims in 'Recovery Position': bodies curled on a floor, legs bent as if the victims were running on a downward slope. The book contained memorably phrased words of wisdom your husband and his underprepared underlings might have done well to heed.

"The time to read these instructions is BEFORE an emergency strikes. Just as the middle of a darkening forest is no place to begin learning to use a map..."

Lucky for underprepared me, one mildly retarded resident of the Group Home crept downstairs, groped mutely in the linen closets for extra blankets. I followed this serenely shuffling resident upstairs, holding the flashlight as she threw blankets over each of the sleeping bodies in the bedrooms. The moans died down at last. I thanked my helper; I told my weary self that I'd done OK, that I didn't smell the adult-shit and baby-powder mix wafting from one room.

After all, everyone in this Home was supposed to be only 'Mildly', right? When my Relief came at dawn, he told me there was in fact a resident in diapers, Phillip, who was only at this Home because his Dad was on the Board.

He shouldn't even be here, this staff member said flatly of Phillip like FEMA spokespeople have said of some victims, like they mean: here on earth.

I wound up bathing Phillip that dawn, being the staff member responsible for his overloaded diaper. It was a small effort that made me feel better, like writing a check or attending a Hurricane Relief benefit or writing these words. At least with Phillip, I did get my hands dirty. A severely retarded man with a baby's sweet fierce stare, Phillip loved to splash his bathwater, no matter what was floating in it.

I learned something about shit that AM, something maybe you know too, Laura. It may be one reason you didn't visit the children and babies of the New Orleans Convention Center.

Because if people are living in their own shit and it's partly your fault, they might just throw some your way. Because, besides: even if you had visited, all you could or would do, really, is shake their hands.

What good is there in that if your hands, our hands, are so cold?

Fruit

by E. Ethelbert Miller

When the dictator opened his eyes
it was early in the morning. There were
several prisoners still waiting to be tortured.

They were in a cold cell hunched over like
bruised apples and plums; their skin peeling
where hands had washed them with pain.

The dictator yawned and scratched himself where
the media could not see. Lately too many things in
the country were going unreported.

No one compiled
the list
of nightmares refrigerated by the police.

The dictator pushed aside his blanket like it was
democracy. His own people were beginning
to leave a bad taste in his mouth. On the table

near his bed an orange was bleeding

Machete Season

by David Mura

I
What I think about now are the comics,
Bikindi, Habimana, who called so cleverly
to kill the cockroaches, so sneaky, so quick,
even my Tutsi neighbors found them funny.

Day after day, over banana beers,
Hutu and Tutsi at the cabaret—
such witty words, such raucous songs--
each laughing at those clowns in our own ways.

*

Grab a machete—that's what we do each morning.
From childhood on. We cut sorghum, prune
banana branches, hack vines, slaughter chickens.
Even women and girls wield it for small things

like chopping firewood. Whatever the task,
the same gesture comes smoothly day after day.
And whether it's cutting a branch, a beast
or a man, well, the blade has nothing to say.

*

Yes, if you must decide yourself, doing in
even some beast can be very discouraging.
But if some authority, if you're not alone....
You go off to it then, you do not worry.

And the Tutsi, their fear was so remarkably clear,
most would just cower or even stand stock still.
And a trembling bleating goat's far more tempting
than one that's frisky, with a spirited will.

*

I'm sure you think I am like the others,
and perhaps I am in so many ways.
You think I am not like you who write this down.
Who lived so far away those killing days.

But if you kill a man, he is still a man.
Whether you call him a cockroach or a friend.
Just as a man who has killed is still a man.
Whether you call him a cockroach or a friend.

II
There's a woman with a jar on her head.
She ambles to the river through the fields.
A mist from off the forest at early morning.
She thinks she will return, her fate unsealed.

And yes, it is this way for many, day by day.
Why would she think there are spirits there waiting?
Or demons or devils? Or simply men,
men who know for her it is already too late.

*

And what if your wife were one of those women?
What if you cannot forget her fine beauty?
She looked at you once in the market and you fell
and only later did you learn she was Tutsi.

But you see, it did not matter then (oh,
perhaps to some but we paid them no mind).
All I knew was that my wife was beautiful,
so patient and generous and kind.

When we left the marsh that first day I'd done nothing.
We passed the house of Abanganyingabo,
a Hutu whom some said had helped the Tutsis:
Behind his house, in a pen, he kept their cows.

"Jean-Baptiste, do you want to save your wife?
You must cut down this cheater here, right now.
Show us you're not like him. Bring us a blade."
The crowd clamored for me to strike a blow.

*

I said nothing to my wife that night in our bed.
I did not reach to touch her, she did not touch me.
Perhaps she was merely tired I told myself.
I had washed in the river, not a stain upon me.

Soon I could tell she was fearful of me.
Perhaps someone had said something, perhaps not.
Everyone knew what we did in the marshes.
Night after night we lay there apart.

III
(And yet I had saved her life, hadn't I?)
I started to stay longer at the cabaret now.
Like others who could not stop their slaughters
I joined in butchering chickens, goats, cows.

Emptying bottle after bottle after bottle.
A man with a pretend smile, a worried ear.
Others went to the woods when their beds went cold.
I tried to tell myself I would never go there.

The rapes came later and spurred men on.
Jealousy spilled from the mouths of Hutu women.
They knew what their men saw in the Tutsi women--
Their slender figures and their smooth light skin.

I told my wife she did not have to worry.
She looked at me, then turned to the wall.
I grabbed her and she slapped my hand away.
"I will not," she said, "sleep with an animal."

*

The Primus, the stolen cow meat and radios;
the bikes, the sheet metal and windows--
people said it was all one lucky season.
There would not be such bounty again.

We had not one wedding or baptism, no service.
We did not care spit for that Sunday silliness.
We were dead tired and greedy. We celebrated.
Anyone who felt sad learned to hide his sadness.

*

One day some drunks came to my door
and shouted I was one of the cheaters.
You are just like Abanganyingabo.
We know you have a cockroach in there.

I looked at my wife and saw it in her face.
I got up and went out into the sunlight.
I walked past the men who shouted my name.
I did not look back when I reached the forest.

History Book

by Ginny Knight

when the pages have yellowed
and the dark words we hurled
     have faded
will some reader turn the
     crackling pages
     and wonder
that we in anger and fear
     turned family
     against family
          our own family
that we in greed and envy
     spoiled air
     and water
          our own land
that we in arrogance
revised ancient truths
     turned away
     those suffering
turned away
     and let starving
     children die

Villanelle for Distant Strangers

by Patricia Monaghan

As strangers suffer, we are distant witnesses
to intimate details of their bodies and their lives
that we should never know. But knowing blesses

us. It makes us sudden lovers. Love caresses
bodies in this way: constant touching with the eyes.
As strangers suffer, we are desperate witnesses

from distant safety. We hear the latest guesses
of fatalities and loss. Each death deprives:
someone we shall never know and knowing, bless.

Yet in their public deaths, each one confesses
more than we might learn in several lives.
As strangers suffer, we are distant witnesses

to their lost hopes and fears and trespasses.
When dreams are drowned, what else survives?
We do not, cannot know. Would knowing bless us

any more than mournful ignorance that compresses
into empathy? The sense of fellowship revives
as distant strangers suffer. We are witnesses.
And those we never knew, unknowing, bless us.

The Planets

by Richard F. Gillum

Wanderers of the night watched
by generations worn, wearied
by the dust of flight,
the scorn upon their head,
the dread played in
their dreams, the penury,
the whimper of children wanting
bread and beds that do not
move from night to night.
Wanderers how can your light
for millennia remain so bright?

Contributor's Notes

Kevin Brockmeier

Kevin Brockmeier is the author of the novels *The Brief History of the Dead* and *The Truth About Celia*, the story collection *Things That Fall from the Sky*, and the children's novels *City of Names* and *Grooves: A Kind of Mystery*. He has published stories in *The New Yorker, The Georgia Review, McSweeney's, The Oxford American, The Best American Short Stories, The Year's Best Fantasy and Horror*, and the *O. Henry: Prize Stories* anthology. He has received the *Chicago Tribune*'s Nelson Algren Award, an Italo Calvino Short Fiction Award, a James Michener-Paul Engle Fellowship, three O. Henry Awards (one, a first prize), and an NEA grant. He lives in Little Rock, Arkansas.

Anne Calcagno

Anne Calcagno received the San Francisco Foundation Phelan Literary Award for stories in her collection *Pray For Yourself* (TriQuarterly Books/ Northwestern University Press), an NEA Fellowship and two Illinois Arts Council Awards. Her fiction has appeared in *The North American Review, TriQuarterly, Denver Quarterly, Epoch*, and other publications, and her stories have been anthologized in the *Penguin Book of Italian American Writing, Fiction of the Eighties, The Milk of Almonds and American Fiction, Vol 2. Out of Noah's Ark* is her first novel. Her nonfiction and travel writing have appeared in *The New York Times*. the *Italian American Historical Society, New City, The Saudi Gazette*, the *Chicago Sun-Times* and *The Chicago Tribune* and *In The Middle of The Middle West*. Calcagno teaches in the MFA in Writing program at the School of the Art Institute.

Bonnie Jo Campbell

Bonnie Jo Campbell writes: I am a writer living in an unfinished house in Kalamazoo, Michigan, with my husband Christopher and other animals. I am six- feet tall and I drive a 1985 Chevy pick-up truck with a rebuilt 350 small-block engine. My first novel *Q Road* was released September 2002 and Kraftbrau Brewery in Kalamazoo has created a specialty beer, Q Brew, to celebrate the occasion. For a while I traveled with the Ringling Bros. and Barnum & Bailey Circus selling snow cones, and as president of Goulash Tours Inc., I have led bicycle tours in Eastern Europe, Russia, the Baltics, and the Balkans. Once upon a time I studied mathematics, but now I mostly write, both fiction and non-fiction but never ever poetry. Occasionally I publish a newsletter, The Letter Parade for my friends and family.

george clabon

George Clabon is from Minneapolis, MN and is Senior Editor of Guild Press. Born in St. Louis, MO, he first moved to Minnesota to attend college. He is the author of several books of poetry.

G.W. Clift

G.W. Clift lives in the Kansas Flint Hills and writes fiction, poetry, and criticism. His story collection is *Mustaches* (BkMk) and a his novel *The Trouble With Campus Security* will appear shortly (from Woodley Press).

Martha Cooley

Martha Cooley is the author of two novels, *The Archivist* and *Thirty-Three Swoons*. She is an Assistant Professor of English at Adelphi University and teaches fiction in the Bennington Writing Seminars.

Philip Dacey

Philip Dacey's most recent book, his eighth, is *The Mystery of Max Schmitt: Poems on the Life and Work of Thomas Eakins*. His latest chapbook, his twelfth, is *Three Shades of Green: Poems on Fatherhood*. More information about him is available on his website: www.philipdacey.com. A longtime resident of Minnesota, he moved in 2004 to Manhattan's Upper West Side. He is currently completing *The New York Postcard Sonnets: A Midwesterner Moves to Manhattan*.

Joe Geha

Joe Geha's work has appeared in various periodicals, journals and anthologies, including *Epoch, The Northwest Review, The Iowa Review, The New York Times, Growing Up Ethnic in America*, and *The Pushcart Prize; Best of the Small Presses*. He is the author of *Through and Through; Toledo Stories*.

Philip Gerard

Philip Gerard is the author of three novels (*Hatteras Light, Desert Kill*, and *Cape Fear Rising*) as well as four books of nonfiction: *Brilliant Passage, a schooning memoir; Creative Nonfiction– Researching and Crafting Stories of Real Life; Writing a Book That Makes a Difference; and Secret Soldiers: How A Troupe of American Artists, Designers and Sonic Wizards Won World War II's Battles of Deception Against the Germans*. He is co-editor with Carolyn Forché of *Writing Creative Nonfiction*. Eleven of his documentary scripts have been produced for public television, and his short stories and nonfiction have appeared in numerous periodicals, including *The New England Review/ Bread Loaf Quarterly, Creative Nonfiction, River Teeth– a Journal of Nonfiction Narrative, Fourth Genre, Tampa Review*, and *Chautauqua Literary Review*. He earned his MFA at University of Arizona and lives in Wilmington, N.C., where he is a professor in the Department of Creative Writing at University of North Carolina Wilmington.

Richard F. Gillum

Dr. Richard F. Gillum, Silver Spring, MD, is a medical researcher for the U.S. government. The author of over 150 articles for scientific journals, he is currently exploring the relationship between successful medical care and spiritual care (including various forms of meditation and/ or prayer). An award-winning poet, his recent poetry looks into the American Indian part of his heritage. (His great-grandfather, the son of a Shawnee woman and a slave in Tennessee, 'borrowed' his master's horse after the Civil War and ran away with his brother to Kansas.) Richard was born in Kansas City, KS, and attended Kansas State University, Justus Liebeg University in Germany, Northern University, and Harvard University.

Dan Guillory

Dan Guillory received his Ph.D. in American Literature from Tulane University in 1972, and began teaching shortly thereafter at Millikin University in Decatur, Illinois. In addition, he has also taught at the University of Wisconsin and Louisiana State University, and he served as a Fulbright Lecturer for the U. S. State Dept. in West Africa from 1989-1990. Mr. Guillory has won awards or grants from the Academy of American Poets, the American Library Association, the Illinois Arts Council, and the National Endowment for the Humanities. In 2004, he was appointed Professor Emeritus of English at Millikin University. He is the author of five books: *Living With Lincoln: Life and Art in the Heartland; The Alligator Inventions; When the Waters Recede; Images of America: Decatur; Wartime Decatur: 1832-1945*. A sixth book, *Macon County*, will be published in the spring of 2007.

William Heyen

William Heyen is Professor of English/Poet in Residence Emeritus at SUNY Brockport. His MA and Ph.D. degrees are from Ohio University. A former Senior Fulbright Lecturer in American Literature in Germany, he has won NEA, Guggenheim, American Academy & Institute of Arts & Letters, and other fellowships and awards. He is the editor of *American Poets in 1976, The Generation of 2000: Contemporary American Poets, and September 11, 2001: American Writers Respond.* His work has appeared in over 300 periodicals including *Poetry, American Poetry Review, New Yorker, Southern Review, Kenyon Review, Ontario Review*, and in 200 anthologies. His books include *Pterodactyl Rose: Poems of Ecology, The Host: Selected Poems, Erika: Poems of the Holocaust*, and *Ribbons: The Gulf War* from Time Being Books; *Pig Notes & Dumb Music: Prose on Poetry* and *Crazy Horse in Stillness*, winner of 1997's Small Press Book Award for Poetry, from BOA; *Shoah Train: Poems*, a Finalist for the 2004 National Book Award, from Etruscan Press; and *The Rope: Poems, The Hummingbird Corporation: Stories*, and *Home: Autobiographies, Etc.* from MAMMOTH Books. Carnegie-Mellon University Press has recently released his first book, *Depth of Field* (LSU P, 1970) in its Classic Contemporaries Series.

Richard Jones

Richard Jones is the author of six books of poems, including his most recent volume, *Apropos of Nothing* (Copper Canyon Press, 2006). His poems are published in such popular anthologies as Billy Collins' *Poetry 180* and Garrison Keillor's *Good Poems*, and he has been heard many times on National Public Radio. In 2000, a volume of new and collected poems, *The Blessing* (Copper Canyon Press, 2000), won the Society of Midland Authors Award for Poetry. For twenty-five years he has been editor of the award winning literary journal *Poetry East*, which celebrates poetry, translation, and art from around the world. Currently he is a professor of English at DePaul University in Chicago, where he directs the creative writing program.

Ginny Knight

Ginny Knight, of Minneapolis, MN, is an award-wining book designer and poet noted both for her strong images and for her sensitivity to 'the others among us'. She was an adult before she learned that she has an Indian great-grandmother. For her long-term dedication to the education of women, believing that the education of a woman means the education of a family, she was in 2006 named a 'Buffalo Elder' by the Oglala Lakota College on the Pine Ridge reservation in South Dakota.

Leon Knight

Leon Knight, of Minneapolis, MN, helped found a small press, Guild Press (of Minnesota), over twenty-five years ago to give voice to poets who were marginalized by mainstream publishers. He likes to tell people, "I got my graduate degree at Harvard and my real education in Africa... Harvard opened certain doors for me, but living in colonial Africa opened my mind and (I Hope) my heart."

John Lane

John Lane has published two full-length collections of poetry, *As the World Around Us Sleeps (1992)* and *Against Information & Other Poems (1995)*. His chapbook, *The Dead Father Poems*, was published by Horse & Buggy Press in 1999. For 20 years he has taught at Wofford College in Spartanburg, South Carolina where he is also one of the founders of The Hub City Writers Project.

Alice Mattison

Alice Mattison is the author of four novels, three previous short story collections, and a volume of poetry. Her work has appeared in numerous publications, *including Best American Short Stories, The Pushcart Prize, The New Yorker, The Threepenny Review, Glimmer Train*, and *Ploughshares*. She teaches fiction in the Bennington Writing Seminars and lives in New Haven, Connecticut.

Cris Mazza

Cris Mazza is the author of a dozen books of fiction, including the critically acclaimed *Is It Sexual Harassment Yet?*, and the PEN Nelson Algren Award winning *How to Leave a Country*. She also has a collection of personal essays, *Indigenous: Growing Up Californian*. The story in this anthology is from *Trickle-Down Timeline*, a collection of fictions due to be published in 2008.

E. Ethelbert Miller

E. Ethelbert Miller is the chair of the board of the Institute for Policy Studies (IPS). He is the author of several poetry collections including *How We Sleep on the Nights We Don't Make Love* (Curbstone Press, 2004). His memoir *Fathering Words: The Making of an African American Writer* was published by St. Martin's Press in 2000. Since 1974 he has been the director of the African American Resource Center at Howard University.

Patricia Monaghan

Patricia Monaghan, one of the leaders of the contemporary earth spirituality movement, has spent more than 20 years researching and writing about alternative spiritual visions of the earth. Raised in Alaska, where much of her family still lives, she considers herself blessed to have learned the ecology of the taiga, the subarctic forest, in her youth. She was a writer and reporter on science and energy-related issues before turning her attention to the impact of myth on our daily lives. Much of her work has explored the role of feminine power in our world, in an inclusive and multicultural way. Her newest book, "*The Red-Haired Girl from the Bog: The Landscape of Celtic Myth and Spirit*," explores the way that Irish mythology expresses the power of the Irish land. She is also an award-winning poet whose work has been set to music and is performed around the world. She has edited two anthologies of contemporary Irish-American writing and is at work on an encyclopedia of Celtic mythology and folklore as well as a book of poems based on Irish myth. Patricia is a member of the Resident Faculty at DePaul University's School for New Learning, where she teaches science and literature. Patricia is a reviewer for *Booklist*, the Journal of the American Library Association.

David Mura

David Mura is the author of three books of poetry, *After We Lost Our Way, The Colors of Desire*, and most recently, *Angels for the Burning* (Boa Editions Ltd.). He has also written two memoirs, *Turning Japanese* and *Where the Body Meets Memory*, and a book of literary criticism, *Song for Uncle Tom, Tonto & Mr. Moto: Poetry & Identity*. His stage work includes *The Winged Seed*, an adaption of Li-Young Lee's memoir, and *Secret Colors*, a collaborative performance piece with African American novelist Alexs Pate. Webpage: www.davidmura.com

Kenneth Pobo

Kenneth Pobo's most recent book, *Introductions*, came out in 2003 from Paerl's Book'Em Press. His work can be read online at journals such as *ForPoetry.com*, *Three Candles, Drexel Online Journal, Big Toe Review, Plum Ruby Review*, and elsewhere. He enjoys gardening, studying Britain's Tudor era, singing along with old Dave Clark 5 tunes, and carnivorous plants.

Frederik Pohl

Frederik Pohl is regarded as one of the greatest science fiction writers living today. His name is synonymous with superb speculative fiction that plumbs the depths of science and politics, and explores man's place in the universe. Lauded as a Grand Master by the Science Fiction Writers of America, Frederik Pohl has had a career in SF that spans over 60 years. He has done just about everything one can do in the field of science fiction, including winning multiple Hugo and Nebula Awards. He is renowned for his wry wit and compassionate satire, and his ability to create mind-expanding worlds. Pohl's Heechee series, which includes *Gateway* and *Beyond Blue Event Horizon* has been the most consistently daring of SF's continuing enterprises. Published in 1977, *Gateway,* the first novel in the series, became a bestseller and won science fiction's triple crown: The Hugo, Nebula, and John W. Campbell Memorial awards for best novel.

Elizabeth Searle

Elizabeth Searle is the author of three books of fiction: *Celebrities in Disgrace*, a novella and stories; *A Four-Sided Bed*, a novel nominated for an American Library Association Book Award and *My Body to You*, a story collection that won the Iowa Short Fiction Prize. Searle's stories have appeared in magazines such as *Ploughshares, Redbook, Agni and Kenyon Review* and in anthologies such as *Lovers*. She has taught writing in the Bennington MFA and Stonecoast MFA Programs. In 2006, she wrote the libretto for an original opera based on the Harding/Kerrigan skating scandal: *Tonya and Nancy: The Opera*. A new production is forthcoming in 2007. She is on the Executive Board of PEN/New England.

Tim Siebles

In addition to his most recent book of poems, *Buffalo Head Solos*, Tim Seibles is the author of *Body Moves*, *Hurdy-Gurdy*, and *Hammerlock*. He is a former NEA fellow and he received the Open Voice Award from the 63rd Street Y in New York City. His work has been featured in anthologies such as *Verse and Universe, In Search of Color Everywhere, New American Poets of the '90's, Outsiders, and the Poets' Grimm*. He has led workshops for Cave Canem—a retreat for African American writers—and for the Hurston-Wright Foundation. He lives in Norfolk, Virginia, where he teaches at Old Dominion University in both their English Department and MFA in Writing Program.

Bob Shacochis

A winner of the National Book Award for First Fiction, the Rome Prize in Literature from the American Academy of Arts and Letters, and a National Endowment for the Arts Fellowship, Bob Shacochis has crisscrossed the globe in his literary pursuits. He graduated from the University of Missouri Journalism School in 1973, and earned a Master of Fine Arts degree from the Iowa Writers Workshop in 1982. A former Peace Corps volunteer in the eastern Caribbean, Shacochis currently teaches in the graduate writing programs at Bennington College and Florida State. He is the author of two short story collections, *Easy in the Islands* and *The Next New World*; a novel, *Swimming in the Volcano*; and a collection of essays about food and love entitled *Domesticity*. His most recent book, *The Immaculate Invasion*, about the 1994 military intervention in Haiti, was recently a finalist for the *New Yorker Magazine* Literary Awards for best non-fiction book of the year, and named a Notable Book of 1999 by the *New York Times*. His op-ed commentaries on the U.S. military, Haiti, and Florida politics have appeared in the *New York Times*, *The Washington Post*, and the *Wall Street Journal*.

Steven Sherrill

Steven Sherrill, Associate Professor of English and Integrative Arts, writes, paints, teaches, and struggles with his banjo, at Penn State Altoona. After receiving a Welding Diploma from Mitchell Community College (and the passing of a considerable amount of time) he went on to earn an MFA in Poetry from the Iowa Writers' Workshop. He is the recipient of a National Endowment for the Arts Fellowship for Fiction in 2002. His first novel, *The Minotaur Takes a Cigarette Break*, is translated into 9 languages. His second novel, *Visits From the Drowned Girl*, published by Random House, US and Canongate, UK was released in June of 2004, and was nominated by Random House for the Pulitzer Prize in Fiction. *The Locktender's House*, novel #3, is due out in Spring 2008.

Barry Silesky

Barry Silesky's collection of short prose, *One Thing That Can Save Us* (Coffee House Press), came out last spring. Many of those pieces have been in various magazines, such as *New Directions Annual, Witness, Fiction, Trafika, Boulevard,* and *Exquisite Corpse*. Silesky has also authored a collections of poems, *The New Tenants* (Eye of the Comet Press, 1992) and a biography, *Ferlinghetti: The Artist in His Time* (Warner Books, 1989). He is editor of *Another Chicago Magazine*, author of a book of short stories out of Coffeehouse Press, and Lawrence Ferlinghetti's biographer. He is also a frequent contributor to Real- Poetik.

Kevin Stein

Kevin Stein's poems and essays have appeared widely in journals such as *American Poetry Review, Boulevard, The Gettysburg Review, The Kenyon Review, Poetry, The Southern Review*, and *TriQuarterly*. His fourth full-length collection, *American Ghost Roses* (University of Illinois Press, 2005), garnered the Society of Midland Authors 2006 Poetry Award. Other collections include *Chance Ransom* (University of Illinois Press, 2000), *Bruised Paradise* (University of Illinois Press, 1996) and *A Circus of Want* (University of Missouri Press), winner of the 1992 Devins Award for Poetry. His prize-winning poetry chapbooks are *The Figure Our Bodies Make* (St. Louis Poetry Center, 1988) and *A Field of Wings* (Illinois Writers, Inc., 1986). Stein's *Private Poets, Worldly Acts*, essays on the interplay of contemporary poetry and history, was published by Ohio University Press (1996) and reprinted in paperback in 1999. That volume earned recognition as an Amazon.com Recommended Book. Stein's *James Wright: The Poetry of a Grown Man* (Ohio University Press, 1989) is considered the definitive study of Wright's work. *Illinois Voices* (University of Illinois Press, 2001), presents an anthology of twentieth-century Illinois poetry which Stein co-edited with G. E. Murray. Stein has received numerous awards, most recently the Vernon Louis Parrington Medal for Distinguished Writing. He has been awarded *Poetry's* Frederick Bock Prize, the 1998 *Indiana Review* Poetry Prize, the Stanley Hanks Chapbook Award, and three Illinois Arts Council Literary Awards for his poetry. In addition, he has been the recipient of the National Endowment for the Arts Poetry Fellowship and three such fellowships awarded by the Illinois Arts Council. Named 1989 Bradley University Professor of the Year for excellence in teaching, Stein is Caterpillar Professor of English and Director of Creative Writing Program at Bradley University, Peoria, IL. In December 2003, Illinois Governor Rod Blagojevich named Kevin Stein the state's fourth Poet Laureate.

Michael Waters

Michael Waters has published eight books of poetry, including *Darling Vulgarity* (2006) and *Parthenopi: New and Selected Poems* (2001) from BOA Editions, and has edited several volumes, including *Contemporary American Poetry* (Houghton Mifflin, 2006). His poems have appeared in *Poetry, The American Poetry Review, The Yale Review, The Kenyon Review*, and *Rolling Stone*. Recipient of fellowships from the National Endowment for the Arts and the Fulbright Foundation, as well as three Pushcart Prizes, he teaches at Salisbury University in Maryland and in the New England College MFA Program.

S.L. Wisenberg

S.L. Wisenberg has published prose and poetry in literary and mainstream publications. She is the author of a collection of fiction, *The Sweetheart Is In,* which was named a notable book of the year by the Chicago Tribune, and an essay collection, *Holocaust Girls: History, Memory & Other Obsessions.* She's the co-director of Northwestern's M.A. in Creative Writing program, and has received grants and awards from the Illinois Arts Council, Fine Arts Work Center in Provincetown and National Endowment for the Humanities.

Paul Zimmer

Paul Zimmer worked for forty years in the book business. He is now retired and lives on a farm in Wisconsin, spending part of each year in the south of France. He has published eleven books of poetry, including *Family Reunion* (U of Pittsburgh Press, 1985), which won an Award for Literature from the American Academy and Institute of Arts and Letters; *The Great Bird of Love* (U. of Illinois Press, 1989); which was selected by William Stafford for the National Poetry Series; *Big Blue Train* (U. of Arkansas Press, 1993); and *Crossing to Sunlight: Selected Poems*, 1965-1995, (U. of Georgia Press 1996). He has read his poems at close to 300 colleges and poetry centers from coast-to-coast, has recorded his poems for the Library of Congress, and has been awarded Writing Fellowships from the National Endowment for the Arts in 1974 and 1981. He has received three Pushcart Prizes and his poems have been widely anthologized. He was the Associate Director of the University of Pittsburgh Press (1967-1978), Director of the University of Georgia Press (1978-1984), and, until his recent retirement, Director of the University of Iowa Press in Iowa City.